Nobody Knows the Spanish I Speak

Laced with rib-tickling cartoons by the author

Applause for
Nobody Knows the Spanish I Speak

"Mark Saunders is the classic American innocent abroad, part clueless tourist, part critic, and always a lover. Humor crackles on every page." *Foster Church, Pulitzer Prize-winning journalist, author of "Discovering Main Street"*

"Thank you, Mark Saunders, for being the one to break out of the rat race, soar off the cliff into the unknown, and live to tell us this heart-warming and hilarious true story. This is one smart, funny, real-life adventure." *Cynthia Whitcomb, TV Writer and Playwright*

"Humorist Mark Saunders has invigorated the memoir form by delivering clever, tightly written comic episodes with hilarity and heart. You'll laugh out loud at these lovable mid-life expats and their eccentric pets." *Kathleen Gerard, award-winning author of "In Transit"*

"If you treasure great American humorists—be they Thurber or Perelman, Barry or Sedaris—you'll love Mark Saunders. His story is a full-course feast for head, heart and funny bone." *Rich Rubin, Playwright*

"Saunders leaves you wanting a sequel. This is one of those books you will laugh along with days after you've finished." *Karen Wallace Bartelt, former newspaper columnist*

"Reading this book is like sitting across from your best friend as he makes you laugh so hard your ribs hurt. Brilliant." *Laurie Halter, President, Charisma Communications*

"Slice the lime, chill the Corona and curl up with Saunders' latest. Every chapter was fresh and LOL." *G.H. Smith, retired business owner and frequent flyer*

"Nobody may know the Spanish Mark Saunders speaks, but *Dios mio*, does he know how to crack wise with the best of them. Take the title. Can't read it without smiling." *Jodi Lustig, Book End Babes Reviewer*

Nobody Knows the Spanish I Speak

Regarding the perils and pleasures of dropping out, selling everything, and moving to Mexico when you're old enough to know better.

Mark Saunders

knishbooks
San Miguel de Allende, Mexico

Knish Books
San Miguel de Allende, Mexico

Nobody Knows the Spanish I Speak Copyright © 2021 by Mark Saunders. All rights reserved. No part of this book may be reproduced, scanned, or distributed in printed or electronic form without permission. Please do not participate in or encourage piracy of copyrighted materials in violation of the author's rights. Purchase only authorized editions.

Book design by Ray Rhamey

ISBN 978-1-7375155-4-8
Library of Congress Control Number: 2011938819

"Yes, We Have No Chihuahuas" originally appeared in *Solamente en San Miguel, Vol. 1, Writings from the Authors' Sala of San Miguel de Allende*. An early version of "How Are Things in Doctor Mora?" appeared as "Say, How's the Foot?" in *Solamente en San Miguel, Vol. II*. Cartoons in this book originally appeared in the panel "Más o Menos" in the weekly bilingual newspaper *Atención San Miguel* and were created by the book's author. Cartoon ideas were contributed by Cliff and Julie DuRand, Vicki Gundrum, Murray and Cleo Kamlehar, and Arlene Lawrence.

for Arlene

Contents

Prologue	2
Salted Omens	12
On the Cuota	26
Starting is Such Sweet Sorrow	38
Scorpions Ascendant	46
Christmas with Bad Santa	56
Yes, We Have No Chihuahuas	68
You Can Call Me Dusty	80
How are Things in Doctor Mora?	90
This Lard is My Lard	100
Mr. Toad's Other Wild Ride	110
How I Learned to Stop Worrying and Love the Firecracker	122
My Body is a Temple That's been Sacked	134
Nobody Knows the Spanish I Speak	144
Waiting for Audi	156
We'll Always Have Parasites	170
I Sing the House Electric	184
Frida's Just Another Word for Nothing Left to Paint	194
Temptation, Thy Name is DVD	204
I Like St. Mike	212
Sometimes Life Really is a Cabaret	222
Love Among the Expats	236
Memoir of an Armoire	250
Epilogue Cassidy Rides Again	266
Postscript	272
About the Author	276
Discussion Guide	278

Muchas Gracias

Wherein I express immense appreciation for my amazing companions on this journey

I want to thank the many wonderful old and new friends who shared in our adventure. The number is too great to list individually by name, but you know who you are. And if you don't know who you are, maybe it's time to consider wearing a name tag, in case you ever get lost or arrested.

I also want to thank the talented, dedicated, hard-working people at FUZE Publishing for allowing me this opportunity: Karetta Hubbard for her wise business counsel and leadership; Meg Tinsley for her astute marketing skills; Molly Best Tinsley and Addie Greene, my editors, for taking the rough clay of my manuscript and molding it into something readable, and, I hope, memorable. And, of course, a big attaboy goes to my book designer, Ray Rhamey, whose imaginative and lighthearted design aptly captures my story.

My sincere appreciation goes to Mexico and the gracious people of magical San Miguel de Allende for tolerating my uninformed ways, silly mistakes, and extremely poor language skills. In spite of everything, you have always made me feel welcome. A tip of my ball cap goes to *La Biblioteca* and Suzanne Ludekens for publishing an amazing and indispensable weekly newspaper, *Atención San Miguel*, and for allowing my cartoons to soak up valuable ad space each week for a year. I offer a special note of appreciation to the talented members of the Literary Sala of San Miguel for their support in publishing two of my chapters while I was working on this book. And *gracias* to former neighbor Bart Briefstein for taking the time to proofread and correct my creative use of Spanish.

I especially want to thank my family. My father, Charles, aka Chuck, who introduced me to humor at an early age, from the funny stories he told to the film comedians we watched together. My mother, Allene, and my sister, Linda, both no longer with us and so dearly missed; each had the kind of warm laugh that could not just fill a room, but also a heart. And I want also to thank my brother, Michael, a guy who knows and loves funny stories. I could not have called God—or Central Casting—and asked for and received a better brother.

Finally, I want to thank Arlene Krasner, my wife, lover, mentor, supporter, boon companion, private chef, and soul mate. Arlene once told me she wanted to be the kind of person she'd like to be best friends with. I'm enormously proud to call her my best friend, as well as my wife. And as a footnote, perhaps most inconceivable of all, she still puts up with my corny jokes and wretched puns, and even occasionally laughs at them. Now *that's* a best friend.

Nobody knows the trouble I've seen
Nobody knows but Jesus

Traditional Spiritual

Nobody knows the trouble with my Audi
Nobody knows but Jesús my mechanic

Mark's Corollary

Nobody Knows the Spanish I Speak

Prologue

 *Concerning the matter of dropping out late in life, why I wrote this book, and what to expect from it, if anything*

A Chinese proverb claims that a journey of a thousand miles begins with one step. Thus our beginnings do not always know our ends.

Put another way, which ragged thread in our lives did my wife, Arlene, and I tug sufficiently to compel us to quit our high-paying, high-tech jobs; to sell our downtown condo with the million-dollar view; to jettison most of our furniture and much of our art, say goodbye to family and friends, load our one remaining car, throw in the cat and dog, and drive south, trading the most livable city we've ever called home for an unknown fate on a dirt road in the middle of Mexico?

Put still a different way, what were we smoking?

The shortest, and perhaps most accurate, answer is to say we were bored with our lives, though comfortable those lives were, felt lost, and wanted to find ourselves again. Then, of course, there were the clichés to consider. Life is short. You only go around once. Seize the day. Do your own thing. Be all you can be. It's a small world after all. We were products of a well-rounded liberal arts education during the rock and roll Sixties and the needles of our lives seemed stuck between the refrains of "What's it all about, Alfie?" and "Is that all there is?"

If most men lead lives of quiet desperation, couples double the ante. We felt it was time, as Joseph Campbell urged, to "follow our bliss."

For Arlene, bliss meant spending more time researching and writing about food, her true passion, and less time worrying about whether a new hardware board for Intel would function as designed. For me, bliss meant more time to write plays and screenplays, as well as drawing cartoons and painting. For both of us, accepting the Call to Adventure at this point in our lives meant dropping out and moving far away.

It's not as if we possessed a greater sense of adventure than any of our Portland neighbors or had been smitten by wanderlust. And it's not as if before moving we had spent any length of time in Mexico or even knew how to speak Spanish. As a college student I once spent a very strange and scary night in Tijuana, the memory of which still induces night sweats. And as a couple we took a cruise that stopped in Cozumel for four hours, where we parked ourselves at a bar and sucked down margaritas until the ship blew its whistle and it was time to re-board. Other than that, Mexico had never registered so much as a blip on our respective travel radar screens.

It would have been safer (and perhaps wiser) to have remained in Oregon and taken the occasional weekend excursion where I would walk out the door dressed like Robert Bly's definition of a modern-day shaman, turn to Arlene, and simply say, "I'm off on a Vision Quest, dear."

She would have replied just as simply, "That's nice, dear. Don't forget your reading glasses." But somehow, not changing our environment when change is what we really craved seemed like going to the Paris Hotel and Casino in Las Vegas when we really wanted to visit Paris, France.

Nobody Knows the Spanish I Speak is dedicated to those who are tired of doing the same thing every day and would like to drop out and try something new. We were. We did. And it changed our lives. We felt, to paraphrase the words of Henry James, "It was time to start living the life we imagined."

Sure, we could have flown to Nepal for two weeks, donned white robes, sniffed incense, crossed our legs, and contemplated our own navels, or someone else's navel. But for all Nepal's natural wonders, we'd heard the restaurant scene there can be disappointing and, like any self-respecting army, Arlene and I travel on our stomachs.

Then a light bulb popped, flickered, and stayed on.

We didn't have to be members of the super rich club or trust-funders or successful software gurus with unlimited shares of hot stock to change our situation. Nor did we have to be life-is-short thrill-seekers, who hang out on the canopy above the Amazon rain forest spotting howler monkeys and swatting bugs the size of King Kong. Or kayak through Glacier Bay blissfully knowing that if a whale breeches nearby and tips the kayak over, we have only ninety seconds before hypothermia sets in. We didn't even have to speak the local language, as long as the local language accepted all major credit cards.

Thanks to a few investments we had a little cash, a nest egg, if you will. We were far from wealthy. But we were in relatively decent health, with the possible exception of higher-than-normal cholesterol counts and blood pressure readings that would be the envy of any bowling league.

In hindsight, it was an easy decision. We were, after all, DINKS—double income, no kids—and had always said if one of us were to raise a hand to say, "Check, please," the other would listen. In this case, after we had both survived multiple high-tech layoffs and downsizings and restructurings and rightsizings and outsourcings and offshorings, we raised our hands at the same time and said, "Enough." Or to give our response the proper cultural spin, *"No más."*

We were ready. It was time. With both our jobs going away and chances of getting rehired slim to none, we decided to drop out of the work force, leave the United States, move to Mexico, and live for a year or two, if not off the lard of the land, at least off part of our savings, since we would have no source of income. Between the two poles of finding one's spiritual self or mistakenly getting one's head blown off in a cross-fire, we felt Mexico had much to offer two inexperienced expats.

Four of us would make the adventure: Arlene, a native New Yorker whose definition of roughing it usually involved ordering the house wine; Cassie, our aging black standard poodle, a girlie-girl who ran side-saddle; Sadie, a part-Siamese cat who believed her reach should never exceed her claws; and yours truly, a neurotic suburbanite from Northern California trying to get by on one forgettable year of high school Spanish. Oddsmakers had the cat down as the one most likely to survive.

Before we knew it we were living in Mexico. The longer we remained there, the more rules we devised to help us define this new old world. We learned to classify our days according to two basic categories. It seemed a day was either a Good Mexico (GM) day or a Bad Mexico (BM) day. We found the vast majority of our days to be GM, but every now and again we'd have a BM. Such is life.

We discovered we were living in a cash-based society where nobody ever had change. In a culture where *mañana* did not always mean tomorrow but could mean anything from later to not now to fat chance you'll ever see me again. In a country where the most common unit of measurement was not the kilo or the kilometer, as guidebooks would have you believe, but something known as *más o menos*, simply translated as "more or less." And no matter where we were in Mexico, it seemed we were always behind a truck.

This book is not about the how-to specifics of retiring in a foreign country, or how much an expatriate should pay for a reliable housekeeper, or where to find the best meals, cheapest rents, coolest night clubs. The publishing world already offers many informative books on those subjects. Nor is it a travel book on Mexico, even though it contains insights and experiences about living in that beautiful, spectacular country. And it's not, as one might expect, a glorious poem to the good life in San Miguel de Allende, where we were to hang our respective sombreros. So many people have already praised San Miguel that even a few of my best adjectives would be either redundant or not up to the task.

Nobody Knows the Spanish I Speak is a story about second chances and personal reinventions, speed bumps and slippery streets, comfortable *casitas* and friendly *tiendas*. It's about the sound of firecrackers going off at three in the morning, and as much about broken-down cars as it is about clear, blue skies as it is about eating corn fungus. Ultimately, though, it's a simple tale about trying something new.

So, what was it like? We loved it. For starters, you can't swing an artist in San Miguel without hitting a writer. And if the writer happens to duck, you'll probably hit a jazz musician. Among its many endearing nicknames, the town could easily add the City of Eternal Memoirs, for there's something about the place that brings out the storyteller in all of us. It could be the striking blue skies, the multitude of historic churches, the colorful houses that make you feel as if you're living in a Mark Rothko painting. Or it could just be having something to say and the time in which to say it.

Truth be told, our lives are stories.

However, the chapters in this book tell our story only, woefully ill-prepared as we were. Other expats, more experienced or wiser, better prepared or financed, and with their own stories to tell, perhaps did not or would not suffer the same slings and arrows, so regularly play the fool, or stumble as often.

Think of any potential mistake an expat can make, and I've already been there and done that. I've said the wrong things, unintentionally, and always seemed to smile at the most inopportune moments. I've referred to women as men and men as women, narrowly escaping a black eye each time. I've over-tipped, under-tipped, and forgotten to tip. I've been given the male hug of friendship called the *abrazo*, as well as the universally recognized middle-finger salute. Along those lines, some of the names in this book have been changed to protect my rental house from a fire bombing. A few locations have been changed as well. San Miguel, however, is still 274 kilometers from Mexico City.

In hindsight, I guess the big takeaway from our story is a twist on that famous saying about New York City: if we can make it in Mexico, anyone can make it.

My goal in writing this book is to share with you our adventure. I hope whatever your primary interest, even if it's as large as an executive class bus or as small as a hairless Chihuahua, there are chapters here for you. And I hope you have as much fun reading the book as I had writing it.

One evening while we were still in our suburban house outside Portland, years before we even considered moving to Mexico, my wife and I were into our cups, drinking wine and listening to soft music, contemplating the pros and cons of downsizing, for we were selling a relatively big house and replacing it with a much smaller condo in the heart of the city. Arlene reminded me that some of our best memories were when we lived in a tiny apartment in New York City.

"That must have been your first husband," I said. "I've never lived in New York."

"Oh, well," Arlene replied. "You know what I mean."

And I did.

Mark Saunders
September 1, 2011
San Miguel de Allende, Guanajuato, Mexico

San Miguel Essentials

Salted Omens

 *Which recounts the three omens I face during the first day of our six-day drive to Mexico and a revelation that results in a last-minute change to our travel plans*

John Steinbeck would have been proud. At least that's what I thought, as I shut the trunk of our 21st century jalopy, a black, four-door, ten-year old Audi Quattro with a matching black luggage carrier on top that looked like a missile launcher. We were minutes away from departing the parking lot of a Starbucks on the corner of NW 23rd Street and Burnside, Portland, Oregon, USA, continent North America, planet Earth for the Promised Land of sunshine in San Miguel de Allende deep in the heart of Mexico. It was a card-carrying December day in the Pacific Northwest: gray, bleak, wet, cold, cruel to asthmatics, and damn hard on arthritics. And if that wasn't enough motivation to put the pedal to the metal and set our compass for warmer weather, it was shortly after six in the morning, as good a time as any to take on rush hour traffic and leave for parts unknown.

If we had gills, we would have been packed to them: two boxes of must-read books, which had been in our condo, unread, for several years but were now deemed, for some lofty reason, indispensable for the journey; a beautiful hardcover copy of a new translation of *Don Quixote*, also, I thought, indispensable; three maps, one each of California, the Southwestern United States, and Mexico; assorted magazines purchased at the last minute; five reams of paper; two printers, one laser and one inkjet; two laptop computers; four pillows; bed linens and a bed comforter; summer and winter clothes, including three changes of shoes, countless pairs of underwear and socks; a survival kitchen set of silverware, pots, pans, cups, glasses, bottled water, even a coffee grinder, enough paraphernalia to outfit a small cabin or a mid-sized sailboat. And in the luggage rack above we stored the double-sized inflatable bed with its expandable metal frame and two inflatable Coleman chairs, our only furniture until the rest of our things, big screen television set and all, were to arrive some two weeks hence at the house we'd rented in Mexico.

In the front seat, we had CDs of favorite tunes to fill the air, books-on-tape to fill the time. But that's not why Mr. Steinbeck would have been proud.

He would have been proud because much like the famed author's tour of America with his poodle Charley, we would be making our trek with a similar dog of great discernment. In the back seat of our car stood—she never sat while riding—a black standard poodle named Cassie.

Beside her nested Sadie, a two-year-old, part-Siamese rescue cat and first-time car passenger in a travel crate, adding still another unknown element to our trip.

Arlene and our friend Mary were already inside the coffee shop, exchanging farewells and drinking a final non-fat cappuccino. I shut the trunk, checked one more time on both pets, took a full breath of tasty Portland air, and looked around at the neighborhood and city that had served us so well for the last twenty years.

Then it happened.

As I tried to make my way back inside the shop, I was accosted by a middle-aged man with a goatee, a stranger in baggy canvas-colored pants, black cowboy boots, wind-breaker, winter scarf, and wide-brimmed hat, the kind of hat one expects to find along the equator on the heads of those who dare to go out in the midday sun. He grabbed me by the arm, gently.

"Hey, Buddy. Can you spare some change?"

I was being panhandled in front of an upscale coffee shop in one of the most gentrified neighborhoods in the entire city, and this before sunrise with Bob Dylan songs piped inside and out.

"Change?" I snapped.

"Yeah, change. I could sure use a cup, man. And at these prices I'm gonna need a couple of bucks. Takes longer than you think to scrape up that kind of cash. Especially this time of day, know what I mean?"

"I think I—" but he beat me to it and finished my sentence.

"—I can tell what you're thinking," he said. "You look at me and you think, 'What's he doing begging for change, man.' Right? Looks healthy enough. No visible scars or wounds. Two arms, two legs. Still got most of his teeth. Sharp dresser."

I wasn't sure about that last point.

"Let me tell you, it wasn't always this way. I used to have a decent job. Got tired of the rat race and dropped out. That's all. Simple as that. Life's too short for that shit, know what I mean. Name's Monty."

Monty shoved his right hand toward me. I shook it as I asked, "You what?"

"Dropped out. You know. Quit the man," said Monty. "Sure, I'm older than most drop outs, so I guess you could say I retired early. Too young for Social Security, too old to get hired. Thought

I'd live off my savings, but that didn't last long. Now I'm out of savings and can't get it together to go back to work. Like I said, life's too short. They can keep that forty hours a week shit. How 'bout some spare change?"

My mouth was ajar; I was all agog and aghast—I'm sure you get the picture. Was I looking at myself in a couple of years when our savings ran out, like a depleted vein of ore, and whatever skills I had that were once marketable were as rusty as the memories of hula hoops and near beer? Would I, too, be hanging around high-end coffee shops begging for fives and tens?

"Yes, I do have change," I said and dug into my pocket, extracting a handful of coins. I dumped the change into his hand, a wad of quarters I was saving for Las Vegas, hoping to squeeze in one last night of gambling on our way south.

"Cool." He bobbed his wide-brimmed head. "Thanks, bro."

"No problem," I said, as he and his hat disappeared inside the coffee shop.

But there was a problem and it was staring me right in the face. The little wheels in my head began spinning out of control. My heart raced and legs wobbled. I felt dizzy and for seconds couldn't focus. It was either the start of a panic attack or that third slice of pizza from the night before. Then I realized what was happening. I had encountered an omen. And it wasn't your ordinary omen, either, considering the circumstances. It was what my friend Jim would have called a "salted omen," the kind that smacked of coincidence, reeked of immediate danger, and is ignored only at one's peril.

"You look like you've seen a ghost," Arlene said.

"I think I did."

"What do you mean?"

"I think I just saw The Ghost of Christmas Future."

"What are you talking about?" she asked.

"I got hit up for change by a man about our age who said he quit work and dropped out, just like we're doing."

I paused for dramatic effect. Both Arlene and Mary looked at me, puzzled.

"And your point is?" Arlene asked.

"I think it might be an omen," I said.

"You're not superstitious are you?" Mary asked.

Arlene looked at Mary, cocked her head in my direction and nodded. "He grew up Catholic, remember?" Arlene replied.

"He's over at the counter getting coffee right now," I said.

We all looked at the counter but he wasn't there. We scanned the room, but he was nowhere in sight. They shot me a suspicious look.

"Maybe he's in the bathroom," I suggested.

"Hmm," said Mary.

"I bought you a double mocha. We should be going," said Arlene.

We said goodbye to Mary, climbed in the Audi, and drove across the street to our neighborhood gas station. Oregon is one of only two states that do not permit customers to pump their own gasoline, so you end up dealing with actual gas station attendants instead of cashiers who just take your money. I thought I knew all the attendants at our local station, but when we pulled up to the pump, a stranger lumbered over. He was a hulk of a man who had been talking to a young woman in black but left her as soon as he saw us.

"Sumtin's wrong with your car," he declared.

"Just want to fill her up," I said.

"Weren't a question, man" he said. "I could hear you from across the street. Sumtin don't sound right."

"Oh, that. It always makes a funny sound in the morning until it warms up," I said.

I opened the car door and got out, handing him my credit card. "Fill it up. Regular, please."

He took the card, ran it through the charge card machine, put the hose in my gas tank, and walked over to the front of the car.

"Pop the hood. I'll check 'er out."

I reached into the car and released the hood latch. He jerked it open roughly and peered in. He stayed under the hood so long I thought he might have fallen asleep or passed out from one too many Hefeweizens, resting his weary head on my engine block. But he popped out suddenly, walked to the side of my car, and finished filling up the gas tank. Within seconds, he was back under the hood, fiddling with something or other, a man on a mission.

He leaned out and shot me a glance. "Go ahead and turn her over. Rev her up a bit."

I crawled in behind the wheel and revved up the engine as requested, which, I had to agree, made a funny noise. But since I'm missing the male car gene, all cars sound funny to me. Love pro football. Love playing poker. Don't get cars.

"What's going on?" Arlene asked.

"Nothing. He heard a funny noise and wanted to check it out."

"It always makes a funny noise in the morning. It's just not an early morning car," she said.

"That's what I told him."

"So why is he looking at the engine? We just had it tuned up by people who actually know what they're doing."

"Better to be safe than sorry, I guess." I knew my answer was lame, but I felt cornered and was only saved from further embarrassment by the attendant. He waved me back out.

"You got yourself a bad water hose, mister. You see this connector here?" He wiggled something, but in the early morning darkness, under the hood of my car, I couldn't see a thing, even under the bright gas station lights.

"Yes," I lied.

"That's gonna give on you first two hundred miles or so."

"I find that hard to believe. We just had the car completely tuned up at the dealership. Put something like five thousand dollars into it."

"Uh huh," he said, unconvinced.

He shut the hood and then stared at me as if I had three horns and wings.

"Where ya heading?"

"Mexico."

"How long a drive?"

"About six days."

"When ya leaving?"

"In five minutes."

This time he looked at me as if I not only had three horns and wings, but also sulfur pulsating from the pores of my skin and nasty big-eyed insects flying out of my mouth. After a pause, he peeked inside the car at my wife, studied the pets, shook his head and looked away, as if he needed to count to ten to control his temper. He was not chewing tobacco, but he spit anyway and turned back to look at me.

"Well, I don't want to say anything bad about dealership mechanics so I won't. Besides, you might make it out of Oregon. You just might." He turned and left.

"We had it checked out at the Audi dealership two days ago," I shouted to his back, as he shrugged and re-entered his cave. The young woman in black scurried behind him.

"We're screwed," I told Arlene.

"What do you mean?"

"The second omen."

"What are you talking about?"

"First the panhandler reminds me of myself. Not a good sign."

"Are you nuts?"

"And now a car mechanic tells us our water hose won't make the trip. We're two blocks from home and we've already had two cosmic nudges."

"Nudges?"

"You know, elbows to the ribs. Wink, wink. How are we ever going to drive three thousand miles at this rate?"

"God, I don't need more coffee. I need a martini."

I knew a third omen must follow soon, for whether we like it or not things in life, both good and bad, come in threes. I don't really consider myself superstitious, at least not in a black cat sort of way, but facts of life are, well, facts of life. There's The Three Muskeeters. My Three Sons. All Gaul is divided into three parts. Old Father William was allowed three questions. The third time is the charm. We're granted three wishes and sing about three blind mice or three coins in a fountain. And, of course, three strikes and you're out.

Omens were piling up like bodies in a Freddy Krueger movie. Nonetheless, with a full tank of gas and keeping an ever-watchful eye out for the next omen, I pulled away from the gas station, cruised along the wet streets of Portland, and eventually found Interstate 5 south. We were on our way. Sunshine here we come, we thought.

On long road trips we usually shared the driving. I would always take the early morning stretch, since all of Arlene's precincts don't report in until around eight or nine A.M. Fortunately, our driving skills complemented each other. I refused to ask for directions, and Arlene had absolutely no sense of direction at all. If Lewis and Clark had used Arlene as their guide instead of Sacajawea, they'd still be looking for the Pacific Ocean. But at least when she was behind the wheel, she paid attention.

On the other hand, I was and am a bored driver, prone to prolonged or even sudden distractions. Driving sixty miles an hour with only a painted line separating our car and a car coming from the opposite direction was not the best time for woolgathering. In fact, life rarely got more existential than that, which was why Arlene was not happy to catch me several times that morning tugging the whiskers on my chin. A true sign of distraction.

"Stop it," she said. "Pay attention."

"You know," I said, changing the subject to show her I was thinking of something important to both of us. "Once we reach Sacramento, we'll be able to give away these bulky winter coats for good."

"I can't wait. Watch the road."

So I watched the road in silence, and it was long and shivering. Not only did Cassie never sit in the car, she had to have her window open the entire way and not a small crack, either. At least half-way down, far enough where she could stick her full head out and, like a vacuum cleaner, suck up all the air around her. We suspect she suffered from motion sickness and the fresh air was the only thing saving our car's upholstery from a fate worse than cat hair. We, on the other hand, suffered from cold and damp weather blowing through the car like a West Coast version of a nor'easter. To compensate, we layered our clothing as if we were Mr. and Mrs. Nanook of the North. We couldn't reach the sunny, dry climate of San Miguel soon enough. In anticipation, I could almost hear the sizzle to come, as years of Oregon rain would leave my body and evaporate into the dry, warm Mexican air. But we had miles to go before we dehumidified.

We drove through the lush Willamette Valley, as the early morning darkness gave way to a lighter darkness generously referred to in these parts as daylight. We passed Salem, Eugene, Roseburg,

Grants Pass, as well as the smaller towns of Drain and Curtin. We stopped for breakfast and for lunch, and along the way we crossed through Oregon into California, whizzed by Yreka, Weed, Shasta City, Redding, Red Bluff, and emerged at the northern end of the long Sacramento Valley. By nightfall we were in Williams, about thirty miles north of California's state capital, and elected to stop at a cheap, pet friendly motel for the night, just off Interstate 5.

Before long Arlene was asleep. The dog and the cat were each as snug as a bug in a rug, as snug, in fact, as the dead cockroach Sadie had discovered earlier in our room. But I couldn't sleep, for the third omen had not yet arrived. I reviewed the events of the day, hoping to find it in some chance encounter. Perhaps it was in the way the waitress in Roseburg continually ignored our request for a coffee refill or the hitchhiker who pulled down his sign the moment he saw us or the guy driving the U-Haul between Ashland and Weed who kept staring at our car and pointing. Before starting out that morning, two strangers had warned me separately about the course of action we were undertaking. Salted omens, no question about it. The warnings were timely. Relevant. Full of danger. All that was missing to make my paranoia complete was unsolicited advice from a blind Greek named Tiresias.

I turned on the television set and there it was, on the screen, before my very eyes, the third omen. It wasn't Tiresias, but it was close enough. It was Albert Brooks in the film *Lost in America*. The movie told the tale of what happened to a married couple after they quit their high-paying jobs, sold their house, said goodbye to family and friends, and drove off into the night in an RV, attempting to find themselves and bring new meaning into their lives.

I watched as Albert Brooks, the husband, learned that his wife, played by Julie Hagerty, had just lost their money in a Las Vegas casino during a frenzied all-night game of roulette, while he was upstairs asleep in their room, visions of self-actualized bliss dancing in his head. She told him that at one point she'd been up three hundred thousand dollars then she'd lost everything, but knew she could win it all back. She just needed a little cash to start again. He struggled to understand. "You mean you lost only the cash we had with us?" "Everything," she replied. All of their cash, then she wrote a check for more money, which she also lost. He finally got it. She lost *everything*, even their all-important nest egg, the financial wherewithal that would enable them to travel the country without having to take minimum-wage jobs or turn into bums. He lectured his wife about the importance of the nest egg, but it was too late. Those eggs had already left the barn. So there they were: broke and jobless and on the road, strangers in a strange land, nesteggless, if you will, bums in the making.

I turned off the television set and sat in the dark for several minutes, chewing on the events of the day as if they were a cheesy plastic straw. Were we destined to become Albert and Julie, only for real and without their Hollywood paychecks or the RV? Then I realized what the universe was trying to tell me. It was suddenly crystal clear. What we were now in the process of doing had nothing to do with one of our ordinary Sunday through Thursday cheap stays in Las Vegas at The Luxor. This was serious stuff. We were not on a part-time vacation. We were on a full-time adventure, moving to another country where we did not know a soul and could barely speak the language.

I turned the light back on, pulled out the map of the American Southwest, and checked the next day's route. Tomorrow, I decided, we would drive through the middle of California, hang a left around Bakersfield, cross the Mojave Desert, and spend the night in Needles. We would bypass the neon allure of Las Vegas, a scant 100 miles to the north, which we had planned to sample for old time's sake. Instead we would stay the course, due south, through Arizona, New Mexico, and Texas. The omens worked. Unlike Albert Brooks, I would be able to sleep through the night and wake up a happy man, with our nest egg still intact. I turned the light off and went to sleep.

An hour later, I was awake again, sitting in the dark and wondering about my chances of finding an Audi water hose in the middle of Mexico.

Major Artifacts of Mexico

On the Cuota

 *In which we make the six-day road trip to the middle of Mexico in winter, during which we lose and recover our vehicle registration just in time to cross the border, and I feud with a cat*

I've been told I'm related to Wrong Way Corrigan, the famous early twentieth century airplane pilot who told everyone he was going to fly solo from New York to California but actually landed in Ireland. Historians believe Corrigan, an expert aviation mechanic, knew what he was doing and had always intended to cross the pond and land in the Old Country, against the wishes of the U.S. government, which had deemed his craft unsafe for a transatlantic flight.

I mention this because we drove from Portland, Oregon, to San Miguel de Allende, Mexico, and didn't, by mistake, end up in Canada. We sallied forth, due south and east and then south again, determined to shed our winter coats and, in the words of the rock musical *Hair*, "let the sun shine in."

Like my ancestor, I had filed a plan. I told Arlene I wanted to be on the road every morning by no later than seven A.M., drive for two hours, stop for a hearty breakfast where, camel-like, we would fill up our humps and continue driving until we reached our destination in time for dinner. Most days, we'd be in transit for ten hours and stop only for gas, twice, and to stretch our legs and let Cassie pee maybe a dozen times. It was what Arlene liked to call a "forced march," but I preferred to think of it as a schedule. My plan's success was predicated on getting an early start, which meant setting our cell phone alarms and the motel room alarm, if it had one, for six o'clock, and making sure everyone was up and about and ready to go, showers taken, car repacked, pets all aboard, Arlene with cup of motel coffee in hand.

Since Cassie had a bladder the size of a caper, my first action item every morning, after turning on the lights and rousing everyone, would be to take her out for a walk. (Sadie's first action item was to run and hide; Arlene's was to complain about getting up so early.) Cassie also had lineage issues and, although hailing from a long line of water fowl retrievers, she detested rain. Some believe the word "poodle" comes from the German *pudel*, for splashing in water. But not our dog. She had evolved beyond such nonsense, and it was absolutely essential for her to find a dry spot, out of the rain, and not near any puddles. Additionally, she was fickle and could change her mind *in media res*. All of which meant a walkie took longer than expected and usually required at least two pick-up bags. Plus, if it was raining, well, then all bets were off.

It rained on the morning of Day Two of our drive. By the time Cassie and I returned from her morning ablutions, it was approaching six-thirty. Arlene, like a good team player, had already taken her shower, dressed, and was packing our things. I'm sure I heard her muttering complaints about the hour, but she came through in the end, and that's what really mattered. While I showered, she made coffee. By seven-oh-five, I was closing and locking the lid of our missile-launcher luggage carrier and Cassie was already inside the car, standing in her reserved rear seat behind the driver. Five minutes late was within the margin of error, and I felt elated. Our clothes, computers, dog food and bowl, cat food and litter box, books and magazines and snacks were all loaded and ready to go. All we had to do was get Sadie into her crate and her crate into the car. And that's when the fun started.

Sadie was hiding under the bed. I crawled on the floor and stared at her. Then, I got a close-up view of the carpet under the bed.

"Don't look under here," I told Arlene. "It's disgusting."

"What's there?"

"Everything, and it's all old and dead. I don't think they've ever cleaned the carpet."

"Gross. What's Sadie doing?"

"Nothing. I think I can reach her."

Belly down on the filthy carpet, I stretched out to grab the cat. But she was outside my reach, and after several minutes of trying I gave up and resorted to Plan B. We tried sweet-talking her.

"Here, Sadie. Come on, girl," said Arlene with the crate open next to her, while I lurked ready to snatch. "Get in the crate. Kitty, kitty, kitty. Come on, Sadie. That's a good girl. Here, Sadie."

Our cat didn't buy any of it. So it was back to Plan A, but this time with a tool. Once again I was on my belly, rubbing my face in God only knew what, and stretching my right arm as far as it would go. This time I used a coat hanger, and this time I touched her. Sadie would just move from one side of the wall to another side of the same wall. After several passes with the coat hanger, I cursed aloud in pain.

"What happened?" asked Arlene.

"I may have pulled my shoulder out."

"Hmm, I doubt it," said Arlene. "I have some ibuprofen in my purse."

I took the pills and opened the motel door.

"Where you going?" asked Arlene.

"No more Mr. Nice Guy," I said as I left the room. I returned minutes later with a long piece of wood that had been discarded in the motel dumpster.

"Get ready to grab her," I said, more determined than ever. I swept under the bed with the lumber, and Sadie ran out, as low to the ground as she could get. Arlene grabbed her, and I held open the crate. We pushed her in backward and locked the crate. By then it was seven-thirty and well outside the margin of error.

"Thanks to that cat, we're thirty minutes behind schedule," I said, as we pulled out of the motel parking lot. It was less than ten minutes later when the second flaw in my morning ritual reared its ugly head.

"Did I lock the luggage carrier?" I asked Arlene.

"I'm sure you did. You lock everything."

"I don't remember locking it. The whole thing could pop open, our stuff would fly out and we'd cause accidents."

"Okay, so pull over and check it."

I pulled over to the side of the road and got out. Arlene was right, of course. It was locked.

We reached our day's destination, Needles, California, just as night was arriving, the four of us and evening checking in at the same time. We upgraded from one queen-sized bed to two queens. The previous night all four of us had slept in the same bed and, this time, we wanted to give ourselves a shot at a good night's rest. As it turned out, we all shared the same bed, again, and the second bed went unused.

In the morning, Day Three, I had steeled myself for what was coming. By seven A.M., everyone and everything was packed, loaded, and ready to roll, all except Sadie.

"Is she under the bed?" Arlene asked, as I crawled around on my hands and knees and looked under both beds.

"Yep. The one we didn't sleep in," I answered. I had a rolled up magazine in one hand and I knew how to use it.

"Is her crate open?" I asked.

"Yes."

I started sweeping the magazine wildly at Sadie. Her head moved to follow each swing. I reached in as far as I could go and lightly slapped the cat with the magazine. She ran out, but Arlene wasn't fast enough and Sadie sprinted under the other bed. I walked over, bent down, and started waving the rolled up magazine at her. She kept scooting away, until I tapped her lightly and she ran back under the first bed.

Arlene tried to snatch her, missed, and banged her shin on the bed frame. This back and forth went on for more minutes than I care to admit. Finally, I had a plan.

"I know what to do," I told Arlene, as I lifted the mattress from the bed Sadie was not under and stacked it in front of its frame, blocking any entrance.

"You chase her out and I'll grab her," I said. And that's how it worked. Who said I'm an idiot?

Arlene swung the rolled up magazine at Sadie, and the cat took off for the other bed, only I was waiting this time. She ran into and then up the mattress, which gave me just enough time to grab her. Seconds later, she was in her crate, while Arlene and I were still huffing and puffing, out of breath.

"I need more ibuprofen," I told Arlene, between gasps.

"What's wrong?"

"I hurt my back lifting the mattress."

We both looked back at the mess we had made of the room. Sheets and pillows were everywhere, and one mattress was tipped on its end. We could have been a minor league rock band on tour.

"Better leave a big tip," Arlene said.

Twenty miles down the road I pulled over to make sure the luggage carrier was locked. It was.

On the morning of Day Four we were leaving Benson, Arizona. Arlene gave me a cup of coffee and two ibuprofens first thing.

Now back to sleeping in a single queen-sized bed, we felt as if we had taken control of the situation. Again, our last step would be to put Sadie in her crate. Rolled up magazine in hand, I looked under the bed.

"She's not there," I said, confused.

"What?"

"Sadie's not there."

"I'll check the bathroom," Arlene said. "You check behind the armoire and chair." But she wasn't there or, as far as we could tell, anywhere in the room.

"Maybe she's in her crate," Arlene said.

"What? You think she turned herself in?"

She wasn't in her crate, either. An unimaginable thought crossed both of our minds at the same time. I said, "Do you think she ran outside when the door was open?"

"She wouldn't do that," Arlene said.

"I wouldn't put it past her. Does she know anyone in Arizona?"

"She's got to be in the room someplace."

"I'll check outside, just in case," I said, walking out the door. Fifteen minutes later I returned *sans* cat, having scoured the parking lot and nearby field. A distraught Arlene sat on the edge of the bed.

"I'm not leaving until we find her," she told me. I rechecked under the bed, behind the armoire, in the bathroom. No cat. I turned on the light to the closet and there she was: Sadie was crouched inside a trough of transparent plastic that served as a tacky storage unit above the closet rod. I could see the shadow of her outline, but she couldn't see me.

Within minutes we were back on the road, and before the first hour was out, true to form, I was on the side of the road making sure the luggage carrier was still locked. It was.

With Sadie's morning disappearing tricks fully anticipated and accounted for, you would think Day Five, beginning in Fort Stockton, Texas, would have started on a more positive note. And it would have, too, except the previous night we discovered we were missing our vehicle registration form, a key document for crossing the border if you want to take your car with you.

"I know I put it in there," said Arlene, meaning our all-important manila documents envelope that included everything from passports to proof of pet vaccinations.

We were on our way to Laredo and had stopped for a substantial breakfast in the small West Texas town of Sanderson, one of many struggling rural towns in the country.

"Maybe we won't need it," I suggested, trying to wear the ill-fitting robe of an optimist. Arlene shot me a double-take, one of her you-must-be-kidding looks. "We can look for it again once we get to Laredo. It's a short drive day, so we'll have plenty of time," I added.

"Hmm," said Arlene. "Why don't we make our own vehicle registration form?"

"What do you mean?"

"Do you know what a Volkswagen Passat vehicle registration form looks like? Or one from Minnesota or Idaho, Vermont?"

"Of course not," I answered.

"Well, the border guards won't know what one from Oregon looks like, either. We have our computers with us."

"Great idea. We can make one up and print it at the library or one of those FedEx Kinko places."

I pulled the car over to the side of the road.

"What are you doing?" asked Arlene.

"I need to check on the luggage carrier. It sounds loose," I said.

On the morning of Day Six, I had set the alarm for five A.M., to ensure we had enough time to reach our destination before nightfall. By seven, we were at the Columbia Bridge border parking lot, a small crossing twenty miles or so west of the main Laredo crossings. The office wouldn't open until eight, so we had plenty of time to think ahead. Ours was the only car in the lot.

A half-hour later, someone tapped on our window and told us if we were planning on crossing into Mexico we needed to be in a different parking lot. I moved our car and, when their doors opened, we were the first ones in. We were ready; unfortunately, they were not. Although the office opened at eight, the woman who made photocopies of the stuff you need to enter Mexico did not arrive until almost nine. We sat inside and waited, stoically, quietly. Until Arlene broke the silence.

"I think it might be an omen," she said.

"What could be an omen?"

"You're early for everything and they're late for everything. I'm guessing you're going to have trouble adapting to life in Mexico."

"Nonsense. I'm very flexible," I said, slightly offended. I stood, yawned, and stretched. "I'm going out for a few minutes."

"What for?" Arlene asked.

"I want to double-check on the pets."

"Uh-huh," said Arlene.

"And the luggage carrier. Make sure it's locked."

Shortly after nine we crossed the border. I handed an official-looking guy the vehicle registration form then set about to look innocent, which wasn't easy as I avoided eye contact. Another official wandered over and the two went into a long pause as they viewed the document, giving our hearts pause, too. Perhaps we misspelled something and they caught it? Not possible. Or it looked too hokey? We reduced it at the copy shop to tighten the text up and make it look professional. I'm not a master forger, but I was proud of the work we did.

Maybe we shouldn't have signed it "Vera Katz," the name of a former long-time mayor of Portland? We never found out why they spent so much time looking it over. It's more likely they were talking about the woman who makes the photocopies. But finally, with a shrug and a wave of the hand we were on our way, inside of Mexico, and headed toward our friend Celia's house in Guanajuato, where we would spend our first night. After that, we'd cruise over to San Miguel and begin our new lives in an old country.

As most travel advisories suggest, we took the toll roads, known as *cuotas*, and found them to be safe and in much better shape than your average American highway. Our trip through the heart of Mexico was a long but uneventful slog, and as darkness fell, we found ourselves walking into Celia's charming house alongside a creek, on land that was once part of a well-known hacienda. Later that night as we walked into her equally charming guest bedroom full of Mexican folk art, I spotted a piece of Nature folk art crawling up a wall. My worst fear was realized—it was a scorpion.

Mexico-savvy Celia came in, said *de nada*, and showed me how to dispatch a scorpion with a shoe. Apparently, the key point to remember when taking on a scorpion, *mano-a-mano*, is to pick up an available, unoccupied shoe and use it to whack the sucker. Never stomp on a scorpion with the shoe that's on your foot, because the scorpion has a better than fifty-fifty chance of winning. She declared our room scorpion-free and we retired for the evening, exhausted after a long day—make that, six days—on the road.

But I couldn't sleep. I waited that night, lying in bed, fully dressed, expecting a foot soldier from the Scorpiones Family to show up and put two in the back of my head.

Indigenous plants of Central Mexico

Starting is Such Sweet Sorrow

 *Which discusses our first impressions, how clueless can we be, and why it took three days to get a set of keys made*

Our rental house was so cold we nicknamed it "The Ice House." It was a charming house and well within our budget, but it was the only place we had ever lived where we had to go outside in winter to warm up. Inside, it was perfect for chilling bottles of chardonnay. Out of doors the temperature ran to the mid-seventies. We initially consoled ourselves knowing we at least had a fireplace. But it took us two days to find wood, and even then it was mass-produced sawdust-pressed logs. Not that it mattered, since whenever we tried to burn one of the "logs," the smoke billowed back inside the house, leaving us in a haze of coughing and the house reeking of soot or whatever glue and sawdust leave in their wake.

In many ways, we were in good company, since most houses in town lacked a heating source other than the sun. However, we apparently had rented one of the seven houses in all of San Miguel that, on average, received less than fifteen minutes of solar energy a day. We feared The Ice House wouldn't warm up until mid-July. Our back courtyard was narrow, faced north, and was shaded by taller houses. Our front courtyard was actually a driveway. Once we tucked our car away inside the gate, there was no room for even a small table and chairs. So, with nowhere else to go, we bundled up inside, supremely glad we still had our winter coats, and shed them only when we went outside.

Fortunately, going outdoors was delightful. Instead of the gloomy, water-soaked skies that lowered over us in Portland, we would look up and see a field of blue, such a deep, intense, magnificent blue that it was easy to understand why even those whose hands had never before touched a red sable brush took up painting once they moved to San Miguel.

On our third day, we rose from our house, left our neighborhood, and took a twenty-minute bus ride into the center of town, for the fare of a mere forty cents. In Mexico, if you want to get from here to there, many people use the bus—it's cheap, it's convenient, and it gets you there on time, usually.

I read that Mexico has the largest bus system in the world, with something like eight hundred different bus companies, and it would not surprise me if that were true. As befitting the largest of anything, the country offers a veritable food chain of buses, from those bottom-feeding ones you see in the movies, with the A-list star balled up between two *campesinos* holding wooden cages of noisy chickens, to high-class luxury buses we only wish we had back in the States.

In between those two extremes sit—or drive—the everyday public buses that ferry residents from one part of a city to another, which is the category of bus we took. It turned out there were two categories of bus travel in town: a bus either had upholstered seats or shock absorbers but never both. The distance between the seat behind you and the one just in front of you provided enough leg room for a Hobbit. And if you were truly adventurous, you took a seat on the spring-less long bench in the back, where you'd feel like a tennis shoe bouncing around in a dryer.

On our initial bus ride into town, Arlene and I sat toward the front, knees scrunched under our chins. The driver's assistant, a young man in his teens, would jump off at every stop and announce the bus and its destination. The bus was nearly full at our stop, mostly with Mexicans, and by three stops later it was packed. Five more expats and several Mexicans got on, including a group of young girls, who scooted to the back of the bus and took over the bench. That's when something happened that I'd never experienced before during a bus ride: the driver pulled into a gas station and filled up. We all waited inside, patiently, and when the driver was ready to pull out, two male musicians with guitars boarded. They strummed and sang their way down the aisle. The young girls in the back clapped to the music, and before we knew it, we were in the middle of a pep rally.

"They must be celebrating something. Do you know what it is?" Arlene asked.

"Our arrival?" I joked, and we laughed.

Soon the bus left the wide, boulevard-like *Ancha San Antonio* and chugged up a steep and narrow street on its way to Centro. We got off the bus in front of *La Biblioteca*, a cultural mecca for expats and Mexicans alike, and slowly walked home from there, taking our time and taking everything in.

When we reached The Ice House, we couldn't find our keys. The landlord had given us only one set of keys to the house, and if we lost the keys—a distinct possibility with our track record—we'd be sleeping in the car. So we did the only logical thing we could do: we panicked. After going through every item in her purse, Arlene finally found our keys, and we found our way inside. Another omen, I wondered?

The next day we set out to get another set of keys made. Simple enough, you'd think. But it took us three days to find the right store to make the right set of keys. And when we did, that same night someone pulled up to our house on a motorcycle, introduced himself as the locksmith who made the original keys to our rental house, and suggested we might want to change the locks. I told him I'd think about it and spent a good part of the night doing just that. When I should have been soundly sleeping, I was mostly awake fretting about the implications of his request.

What did he know that I didn't? Had he already made a hundred copies of the keys to my house and passed them around at parties? Did everybody in the neighborhood have extra sets of keys to our house except us? Once I recalled that the only furniture we had was a metal frame bed with an inflatable mattress and the only valuables were two pets, I decided to ride it out. Living in Mexico was already changing my worry wart DNA.

Sometime during our first two weeks in The Ice House, the water pump, called a *bomba*, died. We didn't know what was going on. All we knew was that it was emitting a horrible, high-pitched sound, a painful and sustained shriek as if the house were passing a kidney stone. We asked the property manager, our warm and effervescent Mexican neighbor, to help. She arrived and unplugged the *bomba*. Cheerfully she said, "Now is fixed." She was correct, of course. The water pump was no longer making a strange noise. It was also no longer pumping water from the street to our tank, and it was only a matter of time before the tank would run dry.

Mere days after we arrived, we ran our microwave and shut down power for the entire street. We called an electrician, who snagged an electric company worker, who shimmied up the utility pole across from our house (without a safety harness) and leaned over to catch tools tossed up by his assistant on the ground. We grimaced with each toss. But all's well that ends well and he fixed the problem—off the books and with a big *propino*, or tip.

Early on we met a fellow expat in our neighborhood, and he asked what kind of visas we had. We proudly said we each had FM3 visas, as opposed to your garden variety tourist visa. The FM3 allowed us to bring in household items and keep our car with our Oregon license plates without having to drive back to the border every six months for renewal. Then he asked if we had registered yet? We learned that even though we had our FM3's, within thirty days we would have to register with *Immigracion*, a government agency, which would require more forms, photos, and money. Fair enough.

Getting our visas wasn't difficult, but it had involved going through several steps with the Mexican Consulate back in Portland. Among other things, we had to get certificates of good health, prove financial independence, and secure a certified letter from the local police department verifying that we had never been featured on "America's Most Wanted." And we had to wait at the consulate to review our paperwork with the powers that be, long waits spread out over multiple visits.

The *Immigracion* clerk in San Miguel politely asked the purpose of our visit. We showed him our FM3 visas and passports. He looked at us and rattled something off in Spanish with the speed of a particle accelerator. We blanched, said nothing. After studying our blank faces for seconds, he handed us a stack of papers, which we took to be an application form, a dense legal document and all of it in inexplicable Spanish. He told us to return the next day.

Dazed, we walked back to our chairs and thumbed through the document, hoping to find a recognizable word or two.

"We are so seriously screwed," I said.

Arlene grabbed my arm and pointed at a woman interacting with another expat couple. We watched as she helped them discuss their situation with the same official. Within minutes the couple signed documents. More minutes later they departed smiling. We rushed up to the tiny woman, introduced ourselves, explained our problem, and threw ourselves on the mercy of her briefcase. Days later, with her help we were street legal.

We celebrated our first week in Mexico with dinner out at a fancy steak house in the center of town. It was not just idyllic, it was romantic. A waiter made a delicious Caesar salad for two, tableside, followed by scrumptious filet mignon steaks with three different toppings, and capped with espresso and flan for dessert.

Afterwards, we walked out into the slightly brisk night air. It was mid-December and a warm, comfortable evening compared to the dreary winter weather in Portland. We ambled, arm in arm, to *El Jardin*, the town's main plaza that faced its most recognizable landmark, a church designed in the architectural style of Gaudi.

We sat on a bench, held hands, and looked up at the night sky. It was a gorgeous full moon, the kind that appears in greeting card photos with captions like "Thinking of you" and travel brochures implying "Don't you wish you were here?" In the background, we could hear a mariachi band playing. A woman with an operatic voice soon joined them and sang what we assumed were love ballads. The park was full of people. Some strolled, some stood, others sat. Everyone listened. Arlene and I were transfixed. We pinched ourselves, for we had landed in Paradise.

Then, out of the corner of my eye, I caught a glimpse of a man in a wide-brimmed hat and baggy pants walking across the plaza. It could have been the panhandler from Portland, Monty, or his evil twin. I would never know for sure. But I took it to be an omen's version of a shot across the bow and, from then on, I made sure to carry a lot of loose change in my pocket.

He must be from Oregon. You can actually hear him dehumidifying.

Scorpions Ascendant

Which recounts my overwhelming fear of scorpions and how, since moving to Mexico, I am finally able to co-exist with those dangerous critters

A month before leaving for Mexico, we were safely ensconced in our Portland condo seven floors above the insects. I was obsessing loudly about scorpions. In thinking back, I see myself in full Napoleonic regalia, pacing from one end of the room to the other, a worried scowl on my face, hands clasped behind my back. Clearly, war loomed on the horizon.

"You're fixating on scorpions," Arlene said. "They're probably not as dangerous as you think."

"Hmm," I said.

Arlene believes the whole point of evolution was to get off the ground and sleep in hotels with clean linen. I think she might be right, but she's also an equal-opportunity bug hater and treats a ladybug with the same disdain as she does a black widow spider. She knew even less about scorpions than I did.

"Why don't you Google them to see what you can find out?"

"Good idea. A little knowledge is a dangerous thing," I replied.

She was right. We'd soon be on the road to Mexico: I needed

to do more research. Besides, it couldn't be as bad as my imagination let on.

It wasn't as bad. It was worse.

I learned that a scorpion is genetically configured with the most menacing traits of a spider, wasp, and lobster without the butter sauce. A scorpion has appendages and pincers sticking out every which way and a poisonous stinger tail that it arches over its back and plunges forward when attacking, much like cracking a whip with laser-point accuracy. It's as if the scorpion was designed, more likely stitched together, during a powerful lightning storm in an underground lab by one of the Christophers, either Lee or Lloyd or Walken—a mad scientist with white hair.

Further, I learned that when a scorpion is hungry it seizes its victim with the pincers, paralyzes it with the stinger, mashes it with its other appendages, injects enzymes into its victim and, once all of the tissues have become fluid, sucks it dry. Sort of like a Slurpee from 7-Eleven. Nothing but the empty carton remains.

What chance do I, a mere human, have against such a formidable enemy, I asked myself? Let's face it, I buy my meat prepackaged at Costco and defrost it in the microwave.

"Scorpions are mostly nocturnal and spend their daylight hours hiding under stones, logs, trash, even beds. They're pretty much loners and usually avoid each other. When they do socialize, it's usually to fight until death, and the loser gets eaten," I told Arlene, as we sat across from each other drinking our morning coffee. She was reading *The New York Times*, a morning tradition for both of us. I, on the other hand, was reading from sheets of information about scorpions downloaded from the Internet.

"Get this. Females often kill the males, and then consume them, after they've mated," I said, amazed.

It was Arlene's turn to say, "Hmm."

"A scorpion can go months without eating," I added.

"What happens if you get stung or bitten?" she asked.

Arlene's use of the word "you" did not go unnoticed.

"Let me see," I said, and rustled through the sheets looking for the answer. "Symptoms include malaise, sweating, heart palpitations, rise in blood pressure, salivation, nausea, vomiting, and diarrhea. You need to get an anti-venom shot within 30 minutes or so. However, you could just as easily react to the serum and suffer blurring of consciousness, unconsciousness, convulsions, a greater fall in blood pressure, shock and, ultimately, death."

I sipped my coffee and thought about it.

"Thirty minutes doesn't seem like enough time," I said.

My wife calmly poured herself another cup as she turned pages of the newspaper. "We'll have our own car down there," she replied.

My education, it appeared, was just getting started. I soon learned that scorpions are one of the oldest members of the arthropod family, spiders and such, with a track record dating back some 430 million years. They can be as small as one-half inch and as large as seven inches, and are found in the desert, savannahs, forests, and, frankly, just about anywhere. Although I found this hard to believe, scorpions have been discovered in such unlikely places as the Himalayas. Scorpions are quite the Sneaky Petes, which didn't surprise me, hiding in places during the day and emerging at night to wreak havoc on the unsuspecting sleeping world with their poisonous stingers.

As if that were not bad enough, I discovered that the average scorpion lives three to five years, but some species can live up to twenty-five years. Those must be the Himalaya ones, I surmised.

"Listen to this," I said, my voice quavering. "More people are bitten by scorpions in Mexico than in any other country. Each year as many as 2,000 deaths occur in Mexico from scorpion bites."

No mention about deaths directly attributed to an irrational fear of scorpions, but that was enough, for I was now over the edge. A little knowledge is a dangerous thing. A lot of knowledge makes for another long string of sleepless nights. I threw my research sheets down in disgust and picked up the front section of *The New York Times*, glad to read about the world's latest man-made catastrophe in the Middle East.

Don't get me wrong: I'm not against defending the homeland from eight-legged invaders. In fact, just two days earlier while reading a book about endangered species, I used the very same book to smash a spider that dared to walk on my floor. As my Uncle Henry would say with a laugh every time a bug hit his car windshield, "I bet he won't have the guts to do that again."

But a scorpion is, well, in a special class almost all by itself, along with most pit bulls, certain species of shark, and the tree-dwelling funnel-web spider—bad apples all. A science program on a cable channel put a scorpion in a glass baking dish and cooked it in an oven at 450 degrees. The scorpion lived. The same program froze a scorpion in a block of ice for two weeks, took it out and let it thaw—it lived.

I understand some Mexicans have been known to keep scorpions as pets. But for the life of me I can't see keeping Skippy around if I'm not sure which one of us, at some future date, will roll over and play dead. Simply put, I had scorpion issues.

As you may have guessed by now, I'm a light sleeper. And the thought of a scorpion scurrying around the beautiful Mexican tiles on my bedroom floor at night or leaping like Spiderman (uh, hello, they're from the same family; it could happen) from wall to wall, didn't help matters.

Although I'm, indeed, a light sleeper, I'm heavy in most other regards. I'm a heavy eater and on the right occasion a heavy drinker.

Largely because of those last two habits, I'm heavier around the middle than I should be or prefer to be. I qualify for the no-neck club because of the heavy thickness of what's just under my face, and my biceps are such that I can generously be described as stocky, even though what used to be muscle has been transformed into flab through the miracle of aging.

I like heavy cream in my coffee, heavy thoughts in my literature, and heavyweight prize fighting. I like heavy desserts and always go for the cheesecake or pecan pie at the expense of more interesting flans or soufflés. I possess a heavy cough, a heavy or deep laugh, a heavy gas pedal, and a heavy dance step—otherwise known as two left feet. Arlene selects a new piece of furniture because it will fit nicely with the décor of a particular room; I reserve judgment until I can see how heavy the piece is to lift.

About almost all things, I come down on the side of heavy except for sleep. I'm arguably the world's lightest sleeper and have been for as long as I can remember. If someone stubs a toe and falls in Singapore, I'm suddenly awake. Like a human dousing stick, I can sense water dripping, in my house or, for that matter, in any house in the entire metro region. I'm a walking—but not sleeping—sensory alarm.

This is not to say I never sleep. I do... but neither deeply nor long enough.

Arlene, on the other hand, has slept through barking dogs, smoke alarms, earthquakes, and helicopters spraying insecticide over our house seeking to eradicate the Mediterranean fruit fly. She once fell asleep while in mid-bite of a burrito. To my way of thinking, it's unfair for a light sleeper, such as I, to be paired up with a heavy sleeper, such as she, but that's the way of the world. While I lie awake, she sleeps peacefully next to me, and, I admit, there's a certain symmetry to the arrangement.

But I was getting cocky about this scorpion business. Nearly a month into our new lives in Mexico and my path had crossed with a scorpion only once, and it didn't end well for Señor Stinger. If it were not for our nightly ritual of checking the sheets and pillow cases, as well as our morning ritual of shaking out our shoes, rituals I introduced, Arlene's protestations notwithstanding, I would not have given scorpions a second thought. In a word, I was adapting.

Then, as they say in fairy tales, something strange happened.

I agreed to meet with a man for breakfast to discuss volunteer opportunities with a local charity. I arrived at the small café early, something one does not do in Mexico, for any reason, which gave my wild imagination time to wildly imagine. Soon a community volunteer named Eric arrived. We introduced ourselves and engaged in the usual chit-chat, shooting the breeze slowly before discussing what *pro bono* work he had in mind.

"Don't anyone move. It's on the floor someplace," a woman's voice boomed.

What's on the floor, I thought? A scorpion? One of them must have followed me here.

Eric was knee-deep into his explanation of the charity, giving me much needed background, and citing examples of how I could help others less fortunate, but I wasn't listening. I was more interested in helping myself. I jumped up, threw down a pocket full of pesos, apologized, and ran for the door, leaving a confused Eric, in mid-sentence, wondering what he had said to offend me. Before I left the restaurant, I heard the woman crawling on the floor speak.

"Found it," she said.

"What was it?" someone asked.

"One of my earrings. It always falls off."

Clearly my life was out of my hands and now controlled by the great arthropods of the earth.

On my way home I concluded I couldn't beat them, so I might as well join them. I rarely sleep anyway, so I decided to become nocturnal and stay up all night, fully dressed and armed, with the lights on and my eyes open. I'd have plenty of time to nap during the day, I reasoned, when we would both be off shift. Local scorpions would be sleeping in their lairs of choice, under rocks and inside of logs, while I would be tossing and turning in my own bed as another sunny day in paradise wafted by outside.

Let's face it, guarding against scorpions is a tough business, but somebody had to do it. I only wished it didn't have to be me.

"Dude, when I'm in San Miguel I feel like I'm living back in the 17th century."

Christmas with Bad Santa

 *Regarding the omnipotent Lord of Customs, what happened to our furniture, the cruel and unusual punishment of sharing an inflatable bed with pets, and how a last-minute vacation to a small town with a friend saved our sanity*

We were on a mission. Climbing through the hills outside the small town of Pátzcuaro, Michoacán, in the central highlands of Mexico, we were driving to the even smaller town of Santa Clara del Cobre, to find the still smaller studio of Ana Pellicer, a copper artist whose work both Arlene and our friend Celia coveted. The geography above Pátzcuaro is much like the foothills of Northern California, a mix of deciduous and evergreen trees towering above wild scrub brush. With an oldies rock and roll station on the radio beaming into Celia's car all the way from Cleveland, USA, courtesy of satellite technology, we could, indeed, have been driving through a hilly section of the Mother Lode country back in the States. Instead, we were in the Sierra Madre mountain range, close to eight thousand feet above sea level, enjoying clear-blue skies and 70-degree weather on Christmas Eve morning. Life was good.

Two days earlier, life was not so good. We'd arrived in San Miguel de Allende early in December but had yet to settle down. We were basically camping, roughing it, inside of our unfurnished and unheated house, and Arlene, especially, is not one for camping. With the exception of an inflatable mattress on a metal frame and two inflatable Coleman chairs, our furniture was in transit and stuck on the road somewhere between hither, thither, and yon. We had nothing more than the clothes on our backs, a few more in our closet, and the "essentials" we'd carried with us in our car during the six-day journey from Portland.

Those essentials included boxes of kitchen utensils (required), boxes of books (optional), and boxes of computer paper (unnecessary), but no real furniture. To make matters worse, the day after the first night in our new residence in Mexico, Sadie, the devil cat, she of the sharp nails, had punctured a hole in one of the Coleman chairs, leaving it more deflated than a Cubs fan and as wrinkled as a Shar-pei. "Chair down," I groaned.

The evenings were much colder than expected, and without central heating or a working fireplace we were forced to bundle up like rural Canadians ice fishing for their supper. When it was time to go to bed, the four of us would end up on the same inflatable mattress on top of a chilly metal frame, struggling to stay warm without moving too much in one direction or the other, for doing so would upset the (un)natural balance of our *ménage au quatre*.

The only way Cassie could get on the bed was to stand in the doorway, start running, aim for the center, and leap as high as she could, like a kid doing a cannonball into a swimming pool. When she splashed down, we splashed up. This pattern repeated itself every night. After the three of us settled down, Sadie would also jump on the bed to complete the foursome. At that point, Arlene and I prayed: *Now I lay me down to sleep and pray the cat her claws to keep.*

If anyone moved, everyone moved. The center of the bed was a dead zone. Roll over and land there and your butt sank to the floor.

Twice a day we called the shipping company responsible for moving our things from the USA to Mexico, and twice a day they told us the same thing: our furniture was at the border stuck in Customs. There was nothing they could do about it. Nothing we could do about it. To give our situation the proper philosophical slant: it was what it was, and it would take what it would take. As each day passed without our furniture, only Customs knew what was going on with our stuff, and they weren't talking. That's when Celia, who lived part of the year in nearby Guanajuato, called and suggested we do what many Mexicans do for Christmas—go to the beach. Celia and her dog, a male apricot-colored standard poodle, arrived the next day, and we left the following morning.

So on the day before the day before Christmas we found ourselves, three humans and two dogs, driving not to the beach, because we couldn't get a reservation at the last minute, but to Pátzcuaro, where we could. Our reservations were outside of the town, in what was referred to as a "rustic" setting. But since the motel had last-minute openings over a holiday, was willing to accept our pets, and offered an unbelievably cheap rate, even by local standards, our "beware of dump" Geiger counters snapped wildly. It was almost Christmas, and visions of a zombie slasher movie danced through my head. En route to Pátzcuaro we elected to skip the cabin and take our chances in town.

As soon as we arrived in Pátzcuaro, Arlene and Celia set out to find new lodging while I walked the dogs. Thirty minutes later, they returned and gave me the thumbs-up sign, to reassure me that our luck would be changing.

We'd all have to share a room and two beds, with each bed on top of its own impressive slab of concrete. After so many uneasy nights spent on an air mattress that wheezed as if it had swallowed a flute, sleeping on concrete seemed downright heavenly. Late in the afternoon, we sat on the large terrace outside our room, sipped wine, and watched nuns, across the way, in their full black and white outfits, as they paced back and forth on the roof of their convent in what I assumed to be their daily vespers. It was idyllic. For the first time in three weeks we were able to forget about the unmanageable demonic force known as Customs.

Prior to leaving San Miguel for Pátzcuaro, I researched our destination and learned the town is one of the most popular places in all of Mexico in which to celebrate the *Día de los Muertos* (Day of the Dead). It has two plazas, several churches, and many fine restaurants and hotels, running from reasonable to less than cheap. *Tiendas* or shops surround the plazas and run up and down the streets. An open air *mercado* takes place beyond one of the plazas, and a smaller open air crafts market operates in a park adjacent to the Basilica, the town's main church. The lower third of the buildings are painted the same brownish-red and the upper two-thirds the same white in the classic Michoacán style.

Pátzcuaro, with sixty thousand residents, is the largest town of many scattered along a lake that has been over-fished. It was established as the religious center of the Purépecha Indian Empire long before the arrival of the Spanish. In the native language, Pátzcuaro means "doorway to heaven."

The Purépecha were long-time enemies of the Aztec and, consequently, joined the Spanish as short-time allies during the conquest. When the Spanish *conquistadors* arrived at Lake Pátzcuaro in 1522, the Purépecha capital was the city of Tzinzuntzan, home for 40,000 indigenous people. However, once the *conquistadors* entered the Pátzcuaro valley, it wasn't long before a greedy, powerful, and cruel *conquistador* plundered and tortured the Purépecha, severely setting back whatever good PR might have previously existed between the conquering and the conquered.

The Catholic Church responded to these barbaric acts by sending a brilliant, compassionate emissary, Don Vasco de Quiroga, who arrived in Mexico in 1530 at the age of 60 (he lived until he was 90 without the aid of either pilates or Ginko biloba). Among Quiroga's many wise moves was to have the Purépecha trained as craftsmen, helping to ensure they could remain independent of the Spanish mine owners, who were also mistreating them. Each village, based on natural skills they already possessed, was taught to master a specific trade or craft.

For example, the residents of Santa Clara del Cobre were trained in the art of copper-making. Pátzcuaro residents were trained in lacquer ware and silver crafts. The village of Tzintzuntzan became known for its potters and basket weavers, the village of Tocuaro for its mask carvers, the village of Janitzio, woodcarving, and the village of Erongaricuaro, weaving. As far as I could tell, the only ones who didn't make a successful go of a special craft learned from the Catholic Church were those poor souls trained to write and speak in Latin.

It was to be our first Christmas as residents of Mexico, and we wanted to make it memorable. We were looking for Ana's copper art, so there was only one place to go.

One glance down the main street of Santa Clara del Cobre explains why it's known as "cobre," for copper studios run through this buyer's paradise like streams through the Rockies. There is a huge town plaque, in copper, of course. As you wend your way through the narrow streets, house numbers are not merely painted on the front or shown in ceramic, as they are almost everywhere else in Mexico, but are hammered out of copper. We first stopped at what was obviously a basic outlet for copper goods: a few good pieces but mostly smaller, more common items, the kind of copper work you could find at almost every store in town. We asked about Ana. The owner knew of her but did not know where her studio was located and did not know of any stores in town that carried her work.

Our next stop was a much bigger and better copper outlet. We'll definitely be able to get directions to Ana's studio here, we told ourselves. The quality of the craftsmanship was higher and the inventory much more extensive. We were invited to visit the *taller*, or workshop, in the back, where we watched an adult male supervise several younger workers, all closer to boyhood than manhood, as they wrestled a huge, rectangular piece of thin copper into and around a crackling fire. One of the workers stumbled briefly into the embers. They tussled with the copper sheet unsuccessfully for several minutes, the smell of burning wood emanated as thick as a fireplace in winter; a bitter-smelling cloud filled the room and our eyes began to tear.

The scene was as comical as it was dangerous. Although we were at the dawn of the 21st century, it could just as easily have been lifted from a B.C. Kodak moment out of the Bronze Age: men playing tug of war with a huge sheet of metal over a roaring flame, without masks, gloves, or tongs. The sign outside the store said "*Hecho Con Mano*" and that seemed to be an understatement, for the goods inside were clearly made by several hands during many attempts to tame the wild beast known as copper. It was an operation that could never happen in America, because it would be in violation of dozens of OSHA and EPA regulations. As we were leaving the store, we asked one of the clerks about Ana P. and, of course, the clerk couldn't help us. If Ana had a studio in town that was open to the public, this store was not aware of it.

We crossed the street to enter a still more impressive copper shop. Their second craft demonstration was more uplifting, even as it smacked of Disneyland. The area where the workers roasted, molded, pounded, then hammered chunks of copper into beautiful vases and bowls and plates and decanters, some decorative and others more functional, was clean and organized. It resembled a museum diorama.

At one end, the oldest man in the group worked a bellows, helping to keep the fire roaring with his consistent rhythm. Young men, in their teens or early twenties, sat off to the side hammering bowls or other items of copper into submission. The tapping was relentless. The next oldest in the group watched a chunk of copper as it roasted in the fire. When it was ready, he removed the chunk and threw it on the ground, away from the fire. At that moment, it was nothing more than a hot block of metal, and what it would become was only in the eye of the artist. He grabbed the copper block with heavy tongs and tossed it on a platform that was not much bigger than the butcher's block in our kitchen.

One man, clearly the leader or supervisor, or perhaps the owner, picked up a sledge hammer and started pounding the metal, flattening it with each swing. The old man working the bellows ran over, picked up another sledge hammer, and pounded. The two of them worked in sequence. Thwack. Pause. Thwack. Pause. Thwack. Pause. Soon three of the younger men joined in with their hammers, and they formed a symphony of thwacks and pauses. The crew's youngest member would hold the metal by tongs and rotate it as the others continued to flatten what moments before was nothing more than a brick-like chunk. They continued to swing the hammer and pound the copper until the block was as flat as the plate that held last night's supper.

On our way out we asked if they knew where Ana P.'s studio was or where we could buy some of her copper goods. They did not know, but they said we might want to try the town's *Museo Cobre*, a museum dedicated to the copper arts. Even there we could not find any information about the elusive Ana P. We returned to Pátzcuaro later that day, with only a few copper items for our efforts and nothing from Ana, not even so much as a studio sighting.

Oddly enough, while window shopping in Pátzcuaro that evening we spotted some of Ana's work and purchased a piece. I hesitated to wax too philosophical, but I thought there was a lesson in there somewhere about traveling so far when what you're looking for is right in front of you. But the lesson didn't rise to omen status, so I dropped the thought, had a beer, and chalked up the excursion as one of my better snipe hunts.

Christmas morning greeted us with a day as clear as any we had enjoyed so far. I was up before the others and decided to fetch coffee for the three of us. We were, after all, in the heart of Mexico, a country known for delicious coffee beans. But it was early on a holiday morning, and I walked several streets before finding a local food shop open for business. By the looks of the place, I could tell fancier espressos and cappuccinos were not going to magically appear in our Christmas stockings. I asked if they served coffee to go, and they did. I wasn't sure about Celia, but I knew from years of experience that Arlene is not a morning person. She doesn't just *like* strong coffee in the morning, she requires it. I asked for three cups of strong coffee, *con leche* on the side since I drink my coffee in the manner known to New Yorkers as "regular," with milk and two sugars. My broken Spanish met the proprietor's broken English halfway, and while waiting for the coffee to brew we had a delightful conversation reminiscent of three-year-olds at daycare meeting for the first time.

Eventually, he brought out a tray with my three cups of coffee. Actually, it was a tray with three cups of boiling water, a spoon, and a jar of freeze-dried instant. To make matters worse, it was decaf.

Hmm, this would not do, I thought. The man who introduced freeze-dried decaf to Mexico should have been boiled in a vat of it. After all, Mexico provides some of the world's best coffee beans.

Later that Christmas day Arlene and I took a stroll around the larger of the two main plazas, where we spotted none other than the American actor Billy Bob Thornton sitting at a small table, having a drink with an artsy-looking gringa. The woman was in an animated discussion with a local vendor, most likely negotiating a better price. Billy Bob watched and smiled. He wasn't laughing or talking. He wasn't doing much of anything. His smile was beatific or cherubic or angelic. Take your pick.

Okay, maybe it wasn't Billy Bob. It most certainly wasn't the even more elusive Ana Pellicer.

But I'd like to think the contented man in the square was Mr. Thornton, and he was neither drunk nor stoned nor sleeping nor otherwise confused or medicated. He wore that contented look because finally, here above the 7,000 foot level, in a modest Mexican town where the simple life is more than a T.V. show and the air is as clean as the sun is bright, enhanced by beautiful hand-made crafts, away from the tacky tabloids and the nosey paparazzi, totally unrecognized, and surrounded by friendly strangers speaking a language he struggled to process—that here, especially here, even a cynical, foul-mouthed Bad Santa could experience peace on earth and good will toward men.

If it wasn't Billy Bob, it should have been. Our first Christmas in Mexico deserved no less.

**Why I Live in San Miguel:
Reason #5**

Yes, We Have No Chihuahuas

 *Regarding the canine species in Mexico and a commentary on how at least some dogs are doing in the central highlands these days*

There are several fine books, chapbooks, and even coffee table books available about the doors, windows, and churches of San Miguel de Allende. But what about the dogs? I asked myself that question as I made my way through the town's small, eclectic bookstore for non-Spanish-speaking types. After all, in the short time we'd been living in that beautiful spot, I'd noticed at least six distinct subspecies or supraspecies of canines. Surely, I thought, these dogs deserve as much attention and photo-spread space as a mere door.

Take *Canis barkus obnoxious*, for example, a mixed breed with an obvious chip on its shoulder. This dog was usually kept locked inside of a *casa* or courtyard, and was always heard but rarely seen. Highly valued by Mexicans and expats alike, especially homeowners of the paranoid sort, this local celebrity dog was worth his or her weight in table scraps. Much cheaper than a home security alarm and consistently more effective, the dog could be found in most neighborhoods, from the center of town to the outlying residential areas. However, if you lived next door to this breed you could kiss a good night's sleep goodbye, for they were relentless barkers. They had one skill, barking, and they knew how to sell it.

A similar breed to your basic courtyard guard dog was *Canis rooftopus*, a subset of highly specialized canines that guarded a house from the roof only. These dogs were always seen and usually heard. Apparently, any size canine qualified for this, ahem, lofty position, and it was not unusual to see two pint-sized terriers working the same roof. Or two German Shepherds. Or a Rottweiler and a Shar-pei. More so than your average guard dog, this breed typically worked in teams of two and three. *Canis rooftopus* was as effective as broken glass cemented to the top of an exterior wall and much more ecologically and esthetically pleasing.

Just below *rooftopus* sat and barked *Canis balconynonus*, typically a breed of a very small type that appeared infrequently at a balcony's iron grill. This dog was clearly well taken care of, preferred to work alone, and only visited the balcony as the mood struck, which meant you had to show ample patience when looking for it. However, a sighting of *balconynonus* was worth catching, for its bark was often both enthusiastic and hilariously high-pitched. If you didn't catch this dog on a balcony, you needn't worry. This species was often seen around town pulling its frustrated owner in several directions.

On the ground was where you usually found *Canis roadkillsimilaris*, otherwise known as the "Is It Still Alive" dog. These dogs were everywhere and resembled some expat retirees in their fascination with *siestas*. *Canis roadkillsimilaris* was the very definition of sloth. In fact, it was often hard to detect if this species of dog was still breathing, short of performing mouth-to-mouth resuscitation on it. This breed was usually found sprawled out in a driveway or on the side of the road. Although *roadkillsimilaris* preferred to sleep in the sun, during the hotter periods of the day or year it usually curled up in whatever shade it could find and considered itself on the job. I'm not sure how or what or when *roadkillsimilaris* ate, since I had never seen any of these dogs actually move other than to swat a fly.

While *Canis roadkillsimilaris* never moved, *Canis wanderlustus* was always on the go. Usually traveling in packs of three or more, *wanderlustus* moved, shark-like, from house to house and neighborhood to neighborhood, searching for food and water. Put your garbage out for collection too soon, and you could bet that *wanderlustus* would find and "trash" your trash faster than you could say, "Beware of dog." Although they often traveled in packs, I never felt threatened by their presence. If I encountered one of these dogs, I simply picked up a rock and pretended to throw it. The dog was sure to leave me alone since this bohemian breed consisted mostly of lovers, not warriors.

The most recent addition to this canine mix, of course, was the transplant known as the expat dog, or *Canis spoiledrottenus*. This breed stood out from the rest by its well-groomed and well-fed appearance, and the confidence the dog had in knowing it would always have "three hots and a cot." Smaller versions of this breed were often carried in Frida Kahlo handbags by senior expat women in wide-brimmed hats. Larger ones grudgingly followed their owners up and down San Miguel's narrow streets.

Our own dog, Cassie, belonged without question to the *Canis spoiledrottenus* camp. She was a nine-year-old black standard poodle who possessed a classy bearing—unlike her owners, who could best be described as a motley crew of two. We would sometimes catch Cassie glancing at us out of the corner of her eye, disapprovingly or condescendingly, as if she were wondering how we ever ended up ahead of her on the evolutionary chart. I often asked myself the same question. With an intense expression on her face, Cassie sat rather formally in a chair, with her front paws crossed and dangling. Her pose was simply regal. She looked as if she were waiting for someone to light her cigarette or peel a grape.

On the other hand, both Arlene and I tended to slouch when we stood, sat, or walked. And when God was passing out tall, dark, and handsome, I was in the men's room taking a whiz. It was not as if Cassie would have ever said anything openly to us about it, even if she could have articulated her disappointment. She was too well-behaved and far too shy to take a public stand, and, as a result, was all the more willing to suffer fools quietly.

We called her Cassiopeia when she was good and Cassandra when she was bad, but most of the time she was just good ol' Cassie, the sweetest dog we'd ever known. When introducing our dog to another dog owner, we would brag that Cassie came before Lassie in the phone book. She was small for a standard, and since I'm never one to pass up a cheap joke, I usually introduced Cassie as being "sub-standard." She seemed repressed, at times, but ran with such enthusiasm that her butt would swing out ahead of the rest of her body, much like a gate swinging back and forth.

She was, to borrow the words of a Tom Robbins novel, skinny legs and all. Whenever three neighborhood Chihuahuas escaped their house during one of our walks, the little yappers went right for her legs. In the scene that ensued, Cassie would watch helplessly, as if the tiny dogs were midget lumberjacks trying to saw her down. It was funny to watch, even if Cassie failed to see the humor in it.

To my larger point, Cassie was not just a dog. She was a girlie-girl who ran side-saddle and walked like Charlie Chaplin in high heels. So I made an effort before we left for Mexico to get Cassie to look like a normal dog. No nail polish. No ribbons or bows. No frou-frou haircuts. Still, I worried that a poodle in Mexico would turn out to be too much of an oxymoron. Worse still, whatever macho points I might have left on the board were sure to be scratched the moment I walked Cassie in our traditional Mexican neighborhood. But the outings were not as publicly humiliating as I had imagined, since most people either weren't out or didn't care. Thus, we quickly settled into a twice-daily routine of "walkies," checking out our neighboring streets together, once in the morning and again late in the afternoon.

We lived in La Lejona, a mostly Mexican middleclass neighborhood with wide, cobbled or unpaved streets, dust everywhere except during the rainy season, and an impressive backdrop of cacti and mountains. The area consisted of about one hundred houses, in various stages of development, from abandoned ruins to brand new structures. La Lejona is Spanish for "far away" and, as I understand it, was the name of the original hacienda in the area, which still exists tucked up against the hillside along a ravine. But far away is a relative term, and our neighborhood was less than a thirty-minute, mostly flat trip into the popular historic Centro on foot, a fifteen-minute bus ride, ten minutes by car or taxi.

Something strange happened one morning during our walk. As always, our first challenge on these walks was to get by two examples of *barkus obnoxious* directly across from our house without creating too much noise. They manned—or dogged—a large, one-level, empty house of brick and wrought iron. One of the dogs was older, a little feeble, gaunt, with skinny legs, and deep-set but very woeful eyes. The other dog was much younger, more energetic, quick to wag his tail, even quicker to snap at other dogs, including his older companion. I named the older dog "Quixote" and the younger one "Sancho."

As soon as we left our house, Quixote and Sancho, without looking up, barked and howled and snarled and carried on as if the entire country were under attack. That is, until they recognized me, and when they did, they quickly replaced their barks with wagging tails. I had been bribing them with treats since our first day in the neighborhood, and, let's face it, a little protection money goes a long way no matter where you are in the animal kingdom.

After leaving Quixote and Sancho, we wandered to the end of our block, turned the corner and headed north. Two of the better examples of *Canis rooftopus* in our neighborhood ruled this street, two dogs I nicknamed Mutt and Jeff, for they were as dissimilar as two dogs could be and still belong to the same species.

Mutt was tall, dark, short-haired, somewhat awkward, and looked as if he could be a little slow on the uptake. He reminded me of the classic dumb-buddy character from the old Saturday morning cartoons. Jeff, his partner in guard duty, was diminutive and light-colored, and moved, herky-jerky, as if he'd been drinking double lattes all morning. He reminded me of the Joe Pesci character in *Lethal Weapon II*. Usually I had to stretch my neck to look up at these two on the roof. Not that day, however. Jeff was on the ground barking and Mutt, still on the roof, was barking back at him. They were oblivious to anyone else around, including Cassie, and were hardly guarding the premises. Instead, they argued back and forth. Although their argument consisted of various barking sounds, in my mind's ear I heard the real story.

How'd you get down there?" barked Mutt.
"I don't remember," barked Jeff.
"You're supposed to be up here with me," barked Mutt.
"No shit, Sherlock," barked Jeff.
"Get back up here," barked Mutt.
"Duh. What do you think I'm trying to do?" barked Jeff.
"Get up here before you get us both fired."
"You see steps? A ladder maybe?"

"How'd you get down there?"
"Don't you ever listen to anything I say?" barked Jeff.
"Get back up here now," barked Mutt.
"What do you expect me to do? Grow wings?"

We left the Bickersons to work out their differences and continued on our walk, heading east up the slight hill. We passed several examples of *Canis roadkillsimilaris* sprawled out in doorways and sidewalks and on the job. They ignored us as we ignored them. At the top of the hill, we turned south, and it was then that we noticed the change. We heard barking from a house that had been previously dogless. Cassie and I looked at each other, confused: tourist or new resident? Just then, a man and his dog emerged from the house. But it wasn't just any dog—it was a small poodle!

The owner, a stocky man a few inches taller than I, approached us with his dog. We stared, smiling, at each other for a moment, standing in the middle of the quiet street with our dogs, bound together in time and space by our walkies.

Me: *Hola. Buenos dias.*
He: *Hola. Buenos dias.*
So far so good.
Me: *¿Estoy bien?*
He: *Bien, bien. ¿Usted?*
Me: *Bien, bien.*
He: *Bien.*
Me: (pointing to his dog) *¿Esta es tu perro?*
He: *Si, si.* (pointing to Cassie) *¿Tu perro?*
Me: *Si, si.*

We stopped talking for a few seconds and looked at each other. Before saying another word, we both knew any conversation beyond this point was problematic. He understood my Spanish would not be up to the task, and I had yet to hear any English thrown my way. So we did the next best thing. We petted each other's dogs for a few awkward seconds and continued to smile.

He: *¿Nombre?*
Me: Cassie.
He: Ahhh. Cussie.
Me: No. KA-sie. Cassie.
He: Ahhh. Cassie.
Me: *Si, si.*
I pointed at his dog and asked its name.
He: *Rocoso.*
Me: *¿Rocco?*
He: No. *Rocoso.*
Me: Ahhh. *Rocoso. ¿Que es?*
He: *¿Como?*
Me: *¿Como se decie in English?*
He: *Rocoso.*
Me: *No comprendre.*

The man started shadow boxing. What'd I say, I asked myself as I ducked? Then he smiled. Raising his arms in the air, in a victory salute, he danced in circles. When all else fails, play charades.

Me: Ahhh. Rocky.
He: *Si, si.* Rocky.

We were done sniffing each other, so it was time to move on. He said goodbye and took Rocky down the street. Cassie and I continued in the opposite direction.

Within the week I noticed two other Mexican families with poodles living on the next street and a great number of poodles in town, mostly the smaller breeds of toys and minis or a poodle mixed with a who-knows-what breed. Suddenly it seemed as if we were in the middle of a poodle population explosion.

It's been said that Americans are appalled at how Mexicans treat their pets and Mexicans are equally appalled at how Americans treat their children. But I'm no longer sure the old clichés still apply. For with Rocoso and others of his breed in the neighborhood and across town, I realized we had a new canine sub-species in our midst. This new sub-species stemmed from upwardly mobile Mexican dog owners who were treating their pets in the well-coddled tradition of their neighbors to the north: professional grooming, long walks, plenty of food and water.

Accordingly, I submit two new classes of dogs be recognized: *Canis gringo spoiledrottenus* and *Canis mexicano spoiledrottenus*. Of course, this meant we now had even more classes of man's best friend south of the border, which was a good thing because, as far as I'm concerned, when it comes to dogs the more the merrier. And that's one post-NAFTA change worth barking about.

Why I Live in San Miguel: Reason #8

You Can Call Me Dusty

Nobody Knows the Spanish I Speak

 *Concerning life in our neighborhood, how we learn to cope with inches of daily dust, avoiding those pesky flying bags of dry cement, and a little more about that little red house we rented*

Even the porn stars were appalled. And they should have been. According to a news story, there was a plan afoot within their industry to start showing adult films in high definition television. Projecting microscopic, crystal clear images of sweaty bodies bumping and grinding, groaning and moaning—an up-close and personal look at warts, moles, zits, nasal hair, varicose veins, bad teeth, old knife wounds, new body piercings, old body piercings, tattoos, and drool—was sure to give pornography a worse name than it already had. I don't care if you're showing Angelina Jolie or Brad Pitt in high def mode, such abnormal clarification is scary and uncalled for.

In my experience, however, nowhere is the close-up more frightening than in an image of your average dust mite magnified ten thousand times. A dust mite so enlarged resembles a man-killer from the covers of 1950s science fiction magazines: its feelers extend in all directions, protruding from a vacuum-cleaner trunk partially covered with follicles that stick out like spikes from Lady Gaga on a bad hair day. Oddly enough, however, a dust mite can't see or bite or drink and lacks a respiratory system. Now you would think with all those limitations—and, I might add, weighing in at a size much smaller than a newspaper's period—the dust mite would be the butt of many late night talk show jokes. Yet it's been around for more than 20 million years, so even your most advanced portable air filtration system from Sears, say, with a successful five-year product record backed by a 90-day warranty, is unlikely to laugh at a dust mite. Which is why millions of those suckers could be sharing your bed with you at night, no matter what precautions you might have taken, and you wouldn't even know it. These dust mite guys are smart and largely go unnoticed. They maintain a low profile by feeding off your dead skin and their own feces, two food groups not desired by anyone else in the food chain. You've got to hand it to them: they found a unique marketing niche and they're milking it for all it's worth.

I knew a little bit about dust mites because I was highly allergic to dust, as was Arlene, as is every member of the human race except three Inuits huddled together on North Baffin Island, and I thought it would be best to know what I was up against. After researching the human-dust mite relationship, it's obvious who's holding the short straw. I give them my dead skin flakes, and they give me uncontrollable fits of coughing and sneezing, red and swollen eyes, itchy skin rashes, a nose that never stops running or is always stuffed, and, of course, a potentially fatal case of anaphylactic shock.

Dust doesn't need mites to do its dirty work, however. Walk outside in just about any town or city and you'll be surrounded by conveyors of dust or, as the professionals like to call it, "particulate matter." You're inhaling every imaginable bit of polluted whatever from asbestos to car exhaust, from lead to dioxin, from paint fumes to tobacco smoke. Put another way, modern man is a two-legged transporter of heavy metals and fossil fuels. Breathing the country air isn't much better, especially when it's loaded with pesticides and herbicides. Stay inside, and even your local librarian could be fast on his or her way to a lung-related illness, because most library books are pretty darn dusty.

All that said and with such a strong aversion to dust, both Arlene and I were surprised to learn La Lejona was a very, very dusty neighborhood. After a few months there, I was convinced it manufactured dust and exported it to the rest of Mexico. Although we knew the guidebooks had referred to the central highlands as "semi-arid," we were hoping for more semi and less arid.

But what did we know? Our first visit to San Miguel occurred over a single afternoon, and we stayed in the non-dusty center of town, where I hunkered down at Harry's, a non-dusty bar, drinking a batch of non-dusty margaritas, while Arlene checked out the non-dusty town plaza. Not exactly a thorough examination, by any standard. On our second visit, the trip during which we rented our first dwelling, The Ice House, we were in town during the tail-end of the rainy season, when signs of dust had been conveniently smothered by waves of precipitation over the preceding weeks. The rainy season here lasts from June through September, *más o menos*. The rest of the year, eight months worth, could be called the dry or dusty season. Therein lies the sneeze.

La Lejona is the kind of Mexican neighborhood where foreigners pat themselves on the back for living among the locals while Mexicans pat themselves on the back for living among foreigners. We wanted to avoid the exclusive gated communities, on principle and because we were working with a limited budget. So we set our sights on a basic, non-touristy, and inexpensive area, and that's how we ended up in La Lejona.

By San Miguel standards it was a fairly new *colonia* and stood out, in part, as being perhaps the only neighborhood within the city limits not to have its own church. But what it lacked in religiosity, it made up for in diversity, and our neighborhood offered everything, including small medical clinics, busy car repair shops, pet care centers, and a raft of home-based restaurants called *casa de comidas*.

We could walk a few blocks to San Miguel's largest grocery store or a little over a mile into the beautiful Spanish colonial center of town. We could even stroll through our neighborhood itself, bounded by cacti and framed by the *Los Picachos* mountains on the east and incredible sunsets to the west.

Although San Miguel sits above six thousand feet, it's considered a part of the low region or "*Baijo*," in these parts, with low being a relative term meaning it's surrounded by higher mountain ranges. During a typical walk through our neighborhood, we would often bump into goats, burros, horses, and dogs, not to mention people—and, as we discovered once we settled in, dust, lots of dust. Except during the rainy season when we had mud, lots of mud.

New houses were added slowly in the neighborhood, since each house was built by hand and only a handful of hands at a time. Rarely is a machine or even a power tool employed. The workers pound one nail at a time. They make their cement in the street, one bag at a time, stirring it like pasta. They first build a wall before knocking a window out of it. On occasion you'll see a head stick out from inside a work-in-progress house, the head's owner having just forced out enough bricks to install a window. If you didn't know better you would think he was escaping from jail.

In short, the act of building one-off houses in La Lejona, as most anywhere in Mexico I imagine, is hard, backbreaking manual labor. But it is, at least, work, and work is hard to come by these days. Did I mention, building a house here also creates dust, lots and lots of dust?

After four months, we moved one street over to a new, small red house with front and back balconies and a see-through wrought-iron gate. Houses are attached to one another and share walls. It's unusual to have a yard in the conventional American sense of the word, but common to a have a courtyard or rooftop terrace, sometimes both. The red house had a courtyard protected by a high wall of bricks covered in a fast-growing, ivy-like plant. Among other plants in our courtyard—and there were many—we had a papaya tree that grew by leaps and fronds. A ceramic tile table for four, with chairs, a barbeque, and an outdoor chimney, along with a water heater, sink, washing machine, and clothesline took up the rest of the courtyard.

Our immediate neighbor to the west was a Mexican family, a young man (an eye doctor) and woman (a dentist) and their two kids. The house on our other side was owned by a family from Mexico City. We always knew they'd arrived for a long weekend when we heard noises on the roof around midnight on a Friday. We'd look out and maybe see their son struggling to get their water or gas tank started. Two new houses were under construction, brick by brick, directly across from our house. An older and larger house adjacent to the new houses sat empty, and next to it were five lots, without houses, all covered in trash and weeds.

If I left our house, turned right, and walked 120 steps, I reached Tony's, a small family-run store. If I left our house, crossed the street, and walked 90 steps, I entered La Ranchita, now closed, a tiny restaurant owned and operated by a young woman, assisted by an older woman who made tortillas to order. In addition to their regular menu, on Wednesdays the restaurant offered what some considered the best *chile relleno* in town. And it was remarkably decent, especially for the price. One time the owner forgot to remove the seeds from the chile pepper and Arlene watched as my mouth visibly melted, like Jim Carey's face in a scene from *The Mask*.

Loose bags of cement flew through our neighborhood like sandpipers on a beach. Thanks to those bags and a windy day, we had as close to a white Christmas as we were ever going to get down there. After returning from a trip to the States, we found our car covered in a thin film of cement. Apparently, the extra cement from the construction site across the street covered our Audi just ahead of a freak winter rainstorm. If we'd been gone any longer, we would have had to chisel our way into the car.

In short, no matter where we walked in La Lejona there was always dust, or particulate matter, natural or man-made. Unless, of course, as I said earlier, we walked during the rainy season. Then we were surrounded—nay, knee-deep—in thick, clay-like mud.

We caught the bug to buy a piece of San Miguel real estate, as almost every expat does after, say, one hour in town. We looked at a nearby neighborhood that was more established, with mostly lush plants and trees, close to a reservoir, and not nearly as dusty. Real estate in San Miguel was, and I imagine still is, evolving. There were no multiple listings. Prices varied from one agent to the next. And the longer a house sat unsold, the more likely it was the owner would keep raising the asking price. It was not unusual for a house to be plastered with half a dozen competing real estate signs, many claiming an exclusive listing. And you had to be extremely careful what you plunked money on and to whom you plunked it. The expat community was full of stories about three different buyers believing they had each purchased the same piece of property. In our brief search, for example, we were shown a piece of property, liked it, and made an offer to purchase. A few weeks later our realtor learned that they had shown us the wrong property and that, although the piece we were shown was indeed for sale, someone else had already *illegally* built on part of it.

We eventually purchased a beautiful corner lot in an area known as Los Frailes, near a body of water, with established houses and gardens and very little in the way of dust. We held off on building a house, eventually sold the land, and stayed put in our initial neighborhood, which we'd come to appreciate in many ways, in spite of the, how shall I put this…*dust*. We compensated by taking more showers than normal, changing our clothes more often, and having our housekeepers clean three times a week, rather than the original once a week. We brought down portable air cleaners, purchased at Sharper Image, and stress tested those babies until they broke. We weren't about to let tiny specks of stuff ruin our stay in paradise.

Living among all that dust brought back an old memory. When I was a reservist in the United States Navy, I spent the occasional weekend or two-week stint on board a ship, usually an oil tanker or a destroyer or a frigate, something uncomfortable that bounced around a lot, even in calm waters. With my active duty experience as a journalist, my reserve time was often spent inside an office, writing and typing reports. Once I was assigned to a burial at sea, back when the Navy was still doing such things. The deceased had been cremated, and we were to cast his ashes into the ocean; I was to witness the ceremony and draft a letter for the surviving family that noted the details of the burial, including nautical coordinates of where the remains were put to rest. Those assigned to serve as the funeral party gathered at the fantail of the ship at the prescribed time. The chaplain said the appropriate words. Appropriate trumpets were played. A flag was just as appropriately folded. Then we were told to scatter the man's ashes, which we did, unfortunately, just as the wind shifted inappropriately. The ashes—I'm sure you saw this coming—ended up not in the ocean but on our clothes and in our faces and hair. For a few minutes at least, the coordinates of the ship were the same as the planned coordinates for the burial, so that was indeed the location I recorded in the official letter sent to the bereaved. The ship's laundry was never mentioned.

My point is, you never know what's in that microscopic speck of dust that just flew into your eye or is now deeply lodged somewhere in your lungs. And you probably don't want to know.

Newbie

How are Things in Doctor Mora?

 *Regarding how San Miguel de Allende became known as the City of Fallen Women and why it has nothing to do with seduction*

I always regretted not buying the first house we almost purchased in Portland. The house was in a small, incorporated area known as Progress, and had we bought it I was looking forward to telling people we lived on the other side of Regress, a missed opportunity to be sure.

When we lived in the central highlands of Mexico, I was surrounded by opportunities equally missed. For example, a few miles from where we lived there was the town of *La Malcontenta*, also known as The Disgruntled Woman, which captured my interest and beckoned my imagination like the sirens of old. I saw it as a town full of wizened widows dressed in black, sitting in the shade on their respective porches, and mumbling prayers as they rolled their fingers nimbly over rosary beads.

My local favorite, though, was the town of Doctor Mora. I'm sure there's a more interesting history behind the name, but to me it conjured up a villain from DC Comics: Batman takes on the sinister Doctor Mora and his deadly radioactive tortilla press in Issue

Number 45. Or, at the very least, if we lived there I could've belted out, in my best faux Broadway voice, "How are things in Doctor Mora?" to Arlene every morning, ultimately turning a basically happy person into *La Malcontenta*.

My point is not to discuss superheroes and villains or even malcontents, but since I wanted to use a title with "doctor" in it, well, there you are. Now that the title is out of the way, I'd like to address the vice president of narrative, the subtitle, and talk about fallen women.

San Miguel de Allende is known as the cradle of Mexican independence and a festival town, as well as an ideal place for artists and art lovers alike. It's also known for its year-around spring-like weather and for its fallen women. Not long ago, the town had its own annual running of the bulls, known as *Sanmiguelada*, and still has its own Mardi Gras-like parade called *Los Locos*. This is a parade where macho men dress up as women and hurl candy with such ferocity and aim that one imagines the entire point of it is to put out as many eyes as possible.

Then there's the local joke—stop me if you've heard this one before—about a man who escapes from prison in the United States and ends up sitting on one of the benches in *El Jardin*, San Miguel's central plaza. A woman sits on the opposite end of the bench and smiles at him. He tries to ignore her, but she's persistent, and finally she asks, "You're new here, aren't you?"

He confesses, "I just escaped from prison."

"Oh," she responds after a short pause, "What did you do?"

"I killed my wife," he replies.

She thinks for a moment and then slides down next to him, smiles, and says, "So, you're single?" San Miguel, as the joke illustrates, is also a town where the female expatriates outnumber their male counterparts by significant numbers.

But until you live in San Miguel you don't fully appreciate why the town is called the "City of Fallen Women," which has nothing to do with the male-to-female ratio or seduction and everything to do with the simple yet painful act of falling down and twisting an ankle and the embarrassment of doing it in public. The streets can be steep and narrow, the sidewalks even more so and, for women especially, the mere act of walking can hold unwanted surprises. Of course, there are the usual signs of dogs doing what they doo-doo so well, requiring pedestrians to look before they step. Buses and trucks can scrape inches off a walker's belly at no extra charge—the distance between vehicles and humans on a typical side street in the historic Centro district is measured in millimeters. Whenever I walked those streets I was reminded of W. C. Fields' claim that it was so crowded at one of his shows the people couldn't laugh "ha-ha-ha," they had to laugh "ho-ho-ho."

For the above reasons and more, a cottage shoe industry sprouted around the treachery of hoofing it about town. Several shops carry what is known as the "San Miguel Shoe." I'm told by women it's that rare fixture in the land of feet: a shoe that is comfortable, stylish, *and* practical. The combination of its rubber soles and thick, elastic straps ensures that the foot stays securely in place, even while your hat and purse fly off down the street in opposite directions. The shoe is available in several bright colors, as well as a classic black, so as you're falling, those watching will be able to compliment you on how nicely your shoes match the rest of your outfit or ask where they might buy a similar pair. Although the San Miguel Shoe may not prevent someone from falling, it could prevent the walker from suffering the further insult of a twisted ankle and, thus, the product has achieved cult status in the town.

Yes, the stones in the street are cobbled, but they're also slippery. So, the smart expat uses the raised sidewalks, also made of uneven stone, as the safest place to put down first a left foot, followed by a right one. This strolling process works well enough until a store vendor casts soapy water in front of his or her doorway to clean the steps, an event that happens with the frequency of a passing cab. If there were a San Miguel Olympics, one popular event would surely be the Doorway Dash, where competitors sprinted in front of soapy doorways, and the one who didn't fall would win.

The streets and sidewalks in the historic Centro can quickly turn a vacation into a hospital visit. Indeed, a common conversation starter is, "How's the foot?" Once you leave the center of town, you do find streets that are both wider and relatively level. Unfortunately, even these streets are unsafe at any speed and sport sudden, inexplicable holes or concrete protrusions in an otherwise smooth surface. So just when you thought it was okay to walk again, even a level street can trip you up faster than you can say, "San Miguel Shoe." What's a walker to do?

Arlene, as a case in point, fell three times during our first two months, and I suspect her number of missteps was about average.

Arlene's first fall came as the two of us were walking home one afternoon from the center of town, leaving the picturesque but narrow streets behind. It was a bright, clear December day and typical of what we would come to expect the longer we remained in San Miguel.

We walked along *Ancha de San Antonio,* a flat, wide stretch of road that morphs into a highway just south of town. Framed by businesses of all shapes and sizes, from hardware stores to fruit and vegetable stands, from roaster chicken shops to espresso hangouts offering free Internet access, even a Ford dealership and a cable television company, the street is like most any other street in any other town or city in North America. It's a street made for walking and, if one gets tired, there's always a steady stream of taxis and conveniently spaced bus stops along the way. We had been in Centro for *la comida*, our mid-day meal, and decided to walk home to work off the calories.

Positioned a few feet ahead of Arlene, I noticed a deep, rectangular-shaped hole in the middle of the sidewalk, bypassed it, and continued on my way. Oblivious as I am, I failed to warn my wife about the hole. Oblivious as she is, she failed to notice it. And to twist a popular quote from the Bible: Obliviousness goeth before the fall. I heard a yell and turned to see Arlene bent over as if she were doing a yoga stretch. Fortunately the hole was neatly shaped to fit her shoe size, which is what we believed prevented her from suffering a more serious injury. She simply fell forward like a cut tree and held that pose. I extricated her foot from the hole. At the same time, a local businessman, seeing the accident, rushed out from his office to help.

Now if Arlene had tripped in the States and a stranger had rushed to her aid, there's no doubt in my mind he would have handed her his card and we would have found a giddy lawyer. But this man's concern was genuine, and after he realized Arlene was able to walk, he hailed a cab for us. As it turned out, she banged her shin, and before long it was the size of a softball. Although bruised and in pain, Arlene toughed it out, took two Advils, followed by a shot of gin, and by morning the swelling had subsided. She was back in the game.

Fall number two was a little more out of the ordinary and occurred at night. Shortly after our arrival in Mexico, friends of friends invited us to their house for dinner. Because we were new to the area and they lived on a steep hill, where we imagined finding a parking spot would be like finding a winning lottery ticket, we took a taxi to their house. We dressed up for the occasion, which for me meant no jeans. Arlene, on the other hand, topped off her outfit with a Mexican shawl known as a *rebozo*. Our hosts lived on a hard-to-find street, and even our driver took a few wrong turns before getting it right. The night was dark, the streets not well lit.

When we arrived, Arlene opened her backseat door and promptly fell out of the cab. Her *rebozo* had entangled with the loose fitting seat belt and tripped her. As she fell to the ground, she struggled furiously with the belt straps much like the Greek statue of *Laocoön* and his sons wrestling with giant sea serpents. I rushed to her rescue. Or rather, I tried to rush to her rescue, but my door wouldn't open, so instead I scooted out on her side, where I, too, fell into the heap that was part Arlene and part seat belt.

The taxi driver rushed to our rescue while apologizing loudly for the accident. I'm not sure if he uttered *"Ay, caramba!"* or *"Ay, chihuahua,"* but I know he said "Ay" several times and followed it with a single word. His mortification was palpable. He untangled us and helped Arlene to her feet, apologized, apologized again, and apologized several more times before going on his way. She sustained a few cuts, a couple of bruises, and a slight limp, most of which disappeared with the morning sun. That was Arlene's second fall.

Proving third time's the charm, it was after Arlene's third fall that we made our first trip to the emergency room at a local hospital. She had volunteered every Sunday for a fund-raiser known as the Home and Garden Tour, where two or three spectacular houses, a different set each week, were open to the public for a small fee donated to a charity.

Arlene's role on that particular day was to help direct a safe flow of people through the house, telling visitors, "You can't go there," or "You've already seen that room," or "Hey, don't use the toilet." She was stationed at House #3 and, at the end of the day's tour, she fell. There's no other way to put it. If the sons and daughters of cobblers go shoeless in the streets, then it's only fair to assume the woman who ensured safe walking would herself trip and fall. Several people rushed to Arlene's aid and helped her get back up, but this time her fall was more serious and, to make matters worse, I wasn't there to help. When she arrived home in a taxi, she was in much pain. We decided this time she needed medical treatment, so off to the hospital we went.

Fortunately, the nearest hospital was just up the hill from our house, less than half a mile, and carried the name of *Hospital de la Fe*, the "fe" of which conjured up historic references to the Spanish Inquisition and left me initially uneasy. Then again, I doubted anyone would go to the local hospital to be drawn and quartered or recant their faith.

In a scene that could have been lifted from an old *Twilight Zone* episode, we entered an empty ER. Unlike in the States, where an average hospital ER would be full of people in all manner of pain and agony, combined with the weeping and gnashing of waiting or filling out admission forms, this room was oddly quiet. The only sound came from a small TV lodged on the wall, where a recent bull-fight gone amuck was on. The bull had escaped into the crowd and gored a handful of surprised spectators. The T.V. station kept re-showing the bull's mad act, as if it were instant replay of an NFL game. Watching the bull flip out and carve up fans, my omen-detector kicked in. What if Arlene needed surgery? Or blood? Or a new foot? *Oy*. Just then, as if on cue, someone came out and handed us a form, totally in Spanish, to fill out. Arlene followed the person inside, leaving me with the form and the prodigal bull.

But "fe" as it turns out means "faith," which is exactly what we had a lot of after our experience. An x-ray, one wrapped leg, a private consultation with the emergency room physician, and a prescription for a pain killer later, we were on our way home. The cost for services rendered by this private hospital? When the evening was over, we were out of pocket approximately seventy-five U.S. dollars for everything.

I've heard expats talk about the miracle of living in San Miguel, most of them referring to the many opportunities for spiritual growth in this beautiful, historic town. I know this will come as a shock since I write much bigger, but I'm a short man. I simply could not afford to spend any time growing spiritually when there was still the potential for an inch or two of physical growth remaining. And let's face it, there's very little that's spiritual about falling on your face in public, especially when sober, for doing so is pretty much a physical act no matter how you spin it.

But when you fall in the street in San Miguel, and you will, there's always someone to pick you up. That's the real miracle of living there.

Proposed SMA Summer Olympics Event #5

This Lard is My Lard

In which I recap the challenges and surprises of cooking and eating in Mexico and make several attempts at eating prickly pear cactus, concluding with a brief look at Arlene's Mexican kitchen, including her wonderful recipe for guacamole

"Do you think people in the Deep South tell strangers that eating okra is like eating cactus?" I asked Arlene.

She put her book down, looked over at me, and sighed. "Where's this going?"

"Everybody here tells me that I should eat *nopal,* and when I ask what it tastes like, they always tell me okra."

"I think okra has a greater slime factor," she said, and returned to reading her book.

"And I don't believe okra has thorns," I added, a key difference to my way of thinking.

"Needles," she corrected. "Thorny needles."

The *nopal* or *nopalitos* paddle, a large, spike-covered extension from the base of the plant, also known as prickly pear cactus, must first be cleaned of its needles before one can eat it. No surprise there. The sharp needles can run in size from microscopic to an inch or so and are not easy to swallow. And that explains why on street corners in San Miguel, you can usually find an indigenous woman removing needles from *nopal* paddles, scraping the cactus clean, and placing it in a plastic bucket, making it safe for resale. If you're a do-it-yourselfer, you can remove the needles with tweezers or that miracle tool of the Adhesion World, duct tape. In either case, it's also a good idea to wear gloves.

Nopals are a staple of the regional diet and rightly so. They are nature's version of a hat-trick, with three-in-one features: a vegetable, fruit, and flower all in one plant. The *nopal* is thought to be native to Mexico and was consumed by locals long before the arrival of Cortez and his armor-plated men on horseback. The scientific name for the cactus plant is *Opuntia ficus indica* and its medicinal qualities are the legendary stuff of both ancient and new-age remedies. *Nopals*, it's said, can help control diabetes and cholesterol while boosting the immune system. Some researchers go so far as to call it a natural hangover cure as well.

Surrounded as the cactus is by unbridled enthusiasm and reverence, I decided to give *nopal* consumption a shot. I went on a self-guided *nopal* tasting and tried the plant in its many edible forms: grilled, baked, fried, in salad, with fruits, and raw. I know the prickly pear cactus is rich in all manner of good-for-you vitamins, but ultimately I couldn't seem to get beyond its taste, which, for me, always landed somewhere between the towns of I Think I'm Going To Gag and Now That's Really Different. Even grilled, generally considered the best way to consume *nopals*, the highly regarded cactus paddle didn't appeal to my taste buds.

But what did I know about food? Truth be told, Arlene is the real food specialist in our marriage. I'm just the eater. And I'm proud of it, too, for a cook without an eater would be like a motorized vehicle without a motor or an actor without an audience or a politician without a lobbyist or a tater without a tot. My point is, ladies and gentlemen of the jury, where would all these fancy television celebrity chefs and their advertisers be without eaters? I rest my fork.

Arlene didn't come by her love and understanding of cuisine easily, however. For the longest time when growing up, she assumed she had been born on another planet and left on her "adopted" parents' doorstep—and this from a girl who never read a superhero comic in her life. It was natural for Arlene to feel like an alien within her own family because she was so different from anyone else around her. She would rather read a book than watch television. She would take herself on long walks. She enjoyed riding the Long Island Railroad train into Manhattan on her own to visit the Museum of Modern Art. And she absolutely loved cooking, still does.

I understood her confusion. After puberty, when my arms began sprouting mounds of hair overnight, I was convinced I was not related to my parents or siblings. Instead, I knew for a fact I was the missing link between ape and man and it was only a matter of time before I'd be featured on the six o'clock news. Then I started going bald: game, set, match. It turned out I couldn't be the hairy missing link after all.

Arlene grew up in a Jewish household that was so Reform she once asked her mother if they were Catholic. Her curiosity immediately landed her in religious training at their local synagogue, where once a week the students made wicker baskets for Israel. Shortly after her arrival, this weekend school raised its rates, and that was the end of her religious training and wicker basket making.

According to Arlene, her grandmother was the world's worst cook. Her Bubbie's matzoh balls would sit at the bottom of one's stomach forever, like fishing line weights snagged on river rock. Her grandmother believed in one spice and one spice only and used it generously: pepper. Whatever was in her kitchen and not moving fast enough, she peppered. If Arlene is to be believed, her grandmother single-handedly introduced into the Five Boroughs the trick of blackening fish and chicken long before fancy Cajun restaurants offered such fare.

One more comment about eaters, and then I'll pass the plate. I'm convinced when Anthony Bourdain goes to that great kitchen in the sky, medical researchers should examine his stomach closely and see how he did it, and perhaps even enshrine his stomach in the Smithsonian. For no matter where he travels, Mr. Bourdain tries the strangest food from the smallest vendor in the middle of nowhere and never suffers the least adverse reaction—at least not on screen. But even though San Miguel has plenty of street vendors, Arlene, a native New Yorker, aptly avers, "I won't even eat from street vendors in New York. Why would I eat food from street vendors down here?"

Much of the food in Mexico is fresh, from eggs to chicken, fruit to nuts. But just to be safe, you must first wash everything with filtered water and soak the items in iodine, especially fruits and vegetables. Although it would be hard to find better asparagus, avocado, or broccoli than what we consumed in Mexico, it was even harder to find an old-fashioned lemon. They sold plenty of *limons* but those were better known in the United States as small limes.

Arlene, as I said, loves to cook and I love to eat, so most of our dining occurred at home, which put unusual pressure on our kitchen, a room in our rental house that brought both good news and bad news. The good news was that we had a gas stove. The bad news was just about everything else about the kitchen. The counters were designed for Andre the Giant. It didn't matter because there was never enough counter space, anyway. The small, single sink was so tiny that if we put three dishes and six pieces of silverware in it at the same time, the water ran over the side and plates begin to rise like ships going through the Panama Canal. Hot tubs in Las

Vegas had more wiggle room. Automatic dish washers were about as common as those real yellow lemons I mentioned.

But I quibble, for Arlene adapted well to her new kitchen environment, and shortly after we arrived, she began cooking local recipes, trying this and testing that. Before long, her kitchen included a *comal*, an earthenware griddle primarily used for cooking tortillas; an earthenware cooking pot, called a *cazuela*, which resembles a bowl with the sides flaring out and a handle on either side of the rim; an *olla*, which is taller and narrower at the top than a *cazuela*, and is used to cook beans; a *cazon*, a two-handled cooking vessel made out of copper; two types of *tortilla press*, one metal and the other made out of wood; and grinding utensils, such as a *molcajete* and its companion *tejolote* (pestle) made of volcanic rock and in an array of sizes. In the words of one of our Mexican friends in San Miguel, Arlene's guacamole tastes "like a Mexican made it." I whole heartedly agree, which is why I've included her recipe in this chapter.

Arlene's Guacamole

Roasting the vegetables gives this guacamole more depth. If you don't have a molcajete (or another mortar and pestle), cut the roasted onion, garlic and chile into a small dice before adding the avocado.
- *3 ripe avocados (preferably Hass)*
- *½ medium onion*
- *1 garlic clove, unpeeled*
- *1 serrano chile*
- *2-3 sprigs cilantro, minced*
- *1-2 limes*
- *salt, to taste*

Heat a comal or griddle over medium heat. When hot, place the onion, garlic clove, and chile on the comal. Turn the vegetables so that they brown on all sides, approximately 15 to 20 minutes. Remove from heat and let cool a little. Peel the garlic clove. Finely chop the onion, garlic and chile.

In a medium-sized molcajete (or a ceramic mortar), grind the onion, garlic and chile to a paste (leave some chunks). A few minutes before you're ready to serve, peel the avocados and mash them in the onion mixture using a fork or the back of wooden spoon. Squeeze a lime or two into mixture and add some salt, to taste. Mix in the minced cilantro—you can save some as a garnish, if you like. You can serve the guacamole right in the molcajete, with some tortilla chips.

While living in San Miguel, I consistently tried *nopals* and, just as consistently, removed those little suckers from my plate. It reached the point where, like a five-year old, I would search out any semblance of a green, chopped-up piece of cactus on my plate and push it over to the edge, out of my harm's way. I had no problems with the rest of the non-American menu items in San Miguel. In fact, I grew to love *chilaquiles*, a breakfast dish that answers the age-old fraternity question: "Hey, what should we do with all these extra tortilla chips?" Put another way, *chilaquiles* is like eating nachos for breakfast. How cool is that? I also ordered and devoured *chile relleno* at many restaurants. Occasionally, I treated myself to a meal of *chile nogales*, a mostly sweet dish that included the colors of the Mexican flag: green (chile), red (pomegranates), and white (sauce). In short, as an eater, there wasn't much I wouldn't try, and usually what I tried I liked.

But I won't eat everything that's put on my plate. I do have standards, low though they may be. For example, it seems as if everyone else in the world loves eggplant but, you know what, I'll pass, thank you just the same. I suppose enjoying eggplant is like enjoying *nopals* and comes under the scientific classification of an acquired taste. The same could be said for the shrimp ice cream sold in the town of Dolores Hildago or the corn fungus speciality, *huitlacoche*, sold in Guanajuato. Both are tastes I may never acquire, even though some consider the corn fungus dish to be a form of truffle. To those misguided souls I say: "I know truffles. Truffles are a friend of mine. And, *huitlacoche*, you're no truffle."

But good things do, indeed, come to those who wait, and I eventually found a *nopal* dish I could tolerate: a *nopal* margarita.

"*Es bueno?*" asked the waiter, after my first sip.

"*Si, muy bueno,*" I answered with a smile. "But next time," I said, "more tequila and less cactus."

"The way I figure it," I told Arlene, "because *nopals* are a hangover cure, I could drink *nopal* margaritas all night and not have to worry about it the next day."

Alternative Use #9 for Nopals

Mr. Toad's Other Wild Ride

 *Concerning the potholes and pleasures of driving a car in Mexico, why the favorite gear in any vehicle is reverse and how come every car has a set of rosary beads dangling from its rearview mirror*

"What do you mean Roberto flunked his Mexican driver's test?"

I was stunned. Roberto was a retired lawyer from the United States. He was also Hispanic and spoke Spanish as well as he spoke English. If Roberto couldn't get a driver's license in Mexico, what chance would I have — a non-lawyer who could barely speak his own mother tongue?

"Well, he flunked the written test, but he paid for the license, so they gave it to him anyway," our friend Celia replied.

"Let me get this straight. As long as you pay for the driver's license, you get it, even if you fail the test?" I asked.

"I didn't even take the test," added an expat eavesdropping on our conversation. "The rules vary from state to state. I just walked in, filled out a form, and paid the fee. Presto. Got my license."

The revelation confirmed what I'd long suspected. Driving in Mexico can be dangerous to your health.

Don't get me wrong. The roads were decent enough, and the drivers courteous enough, and they had easy-to-understand highway signs posted, most of the time, and if you drove only during the day, you could avoid unwanted potholes and undesirable *banditos*, not to mention donkeys napping in the center of the highway, but there was something about driving in Mexico I couldn't put my finger on until that moment.

Nobody was really qualified to drive there, including, or perhaps especially, the expats.

If driving in Mexico turned out better than my worst fears, that only goes to show you how pessimistic I can get. And this broad generalization gives me a lot of room in which to maneuver, more room, in fact, than your typical Mexican road.

The toll roads, marked "Cuota" on maps or road signs, were easier to drive on than most highways in the United States and were not all that expensive, at least relative to what toll roads cost in the States or what I was expecting.

Unfortunately, most of my highway driving in Mexico was on two-lane roads with nothing to stop the on-coming vehicle from hitting me head on, and very little shoulder for a last-second escape. In fact, calling the strip of land that exists between the road and the natural landscape a "shoulder" was often too generous. It was more like a tendon.

Based on my experience, every two-lane highway in Mexico had at least three clearly defined yet invisible lanes: one going in a certain direction, one going in the opposite direction, and the largest lane between the two used by any and all concerned to pass, whether on a curve, hill, or straightaway. And whenever cars passed simultaneously from both directions, which happened more often than the law of averages would seem to allow, you had four invisible lanes in the space of three. During such moments, life on the road was like two demolition derby tracks dropped next to each other, a bumper car enthusiast's dream, to slightly crash the metaphor.

Highway towns controlled the speed of vehicles with *topes*, what up north we called "speed bumps." But where in the USA speed bumps were typically reserved for school and hospital zones and shopping center parking lots, in Mexico speed bumps were everywhere. Sometimes the *tope* was a series of three small mounds; at other times it was a Sierra Madre of hard cement. Usually a highway sign warned you about an approaching *tope* but not always, which is one reason why adjacent to each set of *topes* you could usually find an auto mechanic's shop, a *taller*, specializing in mufflers, tires, and realignments. Next to it, you'd most likely find a small *comercia*, or place where you could sit and eat a meal while waiting for your car to be reassembled. The inverse of the *tope*, the sudden hole in the road, also existed, forcing a driver to remain vigilant at all times.

Roads in the larger towns had something known as a *Glorieta* to offer their drivers. The first time I saw a road sign claim, "*Glorieta*, 300 m," I was on the lookout for some major religious monument. Since it's a beautiful-sounding word and we were living in a country steeped in Catholic heritage, I couldn't help but think *Glorieta* held some angelic or saintly or historic or even civic connotation. As it turned out, a *Glorieta* was commonly known in the road and driver world as a "round-about," the confluence of several roads into one central location.

In other words, it was a traffic free-for-all. At each entrance to the *Glorieta*, an eight-sided, red highway sign with the word *Alto* printed on it stood guard. You could assume that it was a stop sign, and your assumption would be correct. Unfortunately, as I often discovered, *Alto* at a *Glorieta* had a variable highway meaning ranging from the best case interpretation of "Proceed with caution" to the clearly more popular, "You're not a real man if you let someone beat you through this intersection."

Traffic lights were often directly above an intersection, so you had to stretch your neck to see a light change. Street signs were just as often behind trees or walls, almost guaranteeing that you'd miss them. But when you did, there was always a *Retorno* just ahead, a place not far from where you missed your exit and where you could make a U-turn to get yourself back on track. Put another way, a *Retorno* was like the undo button on a computer keyboard.

But just when I thought I understood basic directions in Mexico, I was thrown in another direction. The Spanish word for going straight ahead is *derecho*. Okay, got it. I can understand that word. It's simple. Likewise, the Spanish word for turning right is *derecha*. Works for me. And the Spanish work for turning left is… *izquierda*? Hey, wait a minute. Where'd that word come from? Shouldn't it be "derechi" or "derechu" or some other logical variation on the root word?

Directions were one thing, but vehicles in Mexico were another matter entirely. In my experience, the ultimate driving machine in Mexico had four gears, and each one seemed to be reverse. Of course, that meant you never walked behind either a donkey or a Ford. Small trucks, today's beasts of burden, were often asked to carry loads that even the wisest automobile engineers in Japan failed to anticipate.

It was not unusual to see a load of tree branches or vegetables or furniture extend above, below, and beyond a truck's frame, so that what you saw coming at you was a moving mass of stuff and no visible way for it to be moving. It's said that ants can lift 10 or 50 times their weight. Fleas can jump 100 times their height. Pythons can swallow animals much larger than their own heads. But the Mexican truck, be it a Nissan, a Toyota, or an unidentifiable mash-up of vehicle makes welded together could seemingly do all that and more.

Adapting to the roads, vehicles, and signage was easy. Dealing with the drivers, on the other hand, proved to be more challenging. Mexicans seem blessed with an inordinate amount of patience. They rarely get their dander up or appear uptight or let things, even the little things in life, bother them. Patience is not just a virtue down there, it's the default emotion. When all else fails, it is how you should feel or act or be. You never arrive early for anything. It's always okay to sleep in a little longer or spend more time finishing *la comida*. A shrug is usually paired with *"De nada."* And, of course, there is always tomorrow. We just never knew which tomorrow they were talking about.

I found Mexicans to be patient and easy-going about everything in life. Except driving. I often asked myself: why must they feel this compelling need, such an undeniable itch, to pass another vehicle regardless or in spite of visibility issues?

The first time we were stuck on a two-lane road behind an old truck, bogged to the bottom with its load, indeterminate and indescribable items sticking out every which way, belching more dark clouds than a smokestack in China, a truck last serviced during the Zapata uprising, the answer was obvious: either pass or die of old age waiting to reach your destination. As a result, I learned to pass as I learned to let others pass me.

And yet improbable as it might sound, passing was something of a well-regulated process. Flashing lights behind you meant a driver wished to pass. Flashing lights facing you often meant there was trouble ahead. And if you were in the middle of flashing lights, it was probably too late to do you any good. There were other road courtesies to master. If the driver in the truck ahead of you used his left indicator, it could mean it was safe to pass. It could also mean he was going to turn left. Or, it could mean the truck had faulty wiring. Your guess was as good as theirs.

Octavio Paz, the Latin American literary giant, said that Mexicans never forget their past. I believe what he really meant to say was that Mexicans never forget *to pass*.

Once a month we were able to apply what driving lessons we had learned when we did what was commonly referred to as a "Costco run." Although San Miguel offered modest stores and shops, two nearby bigger cities, Celaya and Queretaro, were similar to American cities of like size and included modern shopping conveniences, from a Costco to an Office Depot to a Sears. Making a Costco run provided us an opportunity to take the Audi on the road and blow it out, as they say, while we stocked up on staples, such as paper goods, meats, office materials, and the like. Celaya was about a thirty-minute drive due south of San Miguel; Queretaro closer to forty-five minutes east of where we lived. On one Costco run in particular we elected to go to Celaya.

The road south out of San Miguel climbed quickly through a mountain pass and, once you began your ascent, you always found yourself moving at a snail's pace, following in the wake of a much bigger and slower snail. After you reached the crest, you'd get a better view of the downhill passage on the other side, a road with hairpin curves, no shoulder, and a sure drop to the bottom that warned some drivers about passing and encouraged others to do so. It was usually at this point where Arlene would remind me we were in no hurry and to let other cars pass if they wished. I did. And against my better male instincts, I wouldn't pass.

What I often did, though, was miss the bypass, forcing us to drive through the town of Comonfort, a small town perhaps best known for its sidewalk kitchen wares and, the town's crown jewel, a custom-made furniture store. Along the main road through the town, we'd see a vast array of strange, brightly colored objects for sale, the kind of stuff one could win at a traveling carnival.

Comonfort was also well known for the height and frequency of its *topes*. Moving through town, I drove slowly over each and every speed bump, hearing the painful scraping sounds of my car, groaning like an unranked prize fighter taking a pounding to the midsection in the late rounds, until we reconnected with the main highway.

Entering Celaya from the north required crossing a busy *Glorieta*, one of the more dangerous ones in my experience, that was always frantic with container trucks, buses, smaller trucks, and cars, all vying in a clear violation of the laws of physics for the same lane at the exact same time. On this trip, when we approached the round-about, we saw a car to our left, recently overturned, and sitting like a powerless potato bug upside down on its own shell. Police and traffic enforcers worked the scene, and no one seemed worse for wear except me because, of course, I saw it as an omen.

We arrived at Costco, shopped, had the obligatory hot dog and soda for lunch, and headed home. On our return trip, taking advantage of a long, even stretch of road that ended in a slight rise, I put the pedal to the metal and increased my speed. Suddenly, from the top of the approaching rise, a semi-tractor trailer appeared heading toward me, which, in many ways, was to be expected and certainly not out of the ordinary. What was unexpected, however, were the two other semi-tractor trailers, each from the same long-haul firm, and each passing the other trailer by way of my lane.

Many years ago when I was in the United States Navy and assigned to the Seabees, the Navy's construction outfit, I was stationed at Roosevelt Roads on Puerto Rico for nine months. During part of that time, several of my friends were assigned to a small detachment working on a mountaintop in St. Thomas, Virgin Islands, sent there to build a satellite station, as I recall. One Saturday night two of my friends in the detachment checked out a truck from the battalion motor pool and headed down the mountain to the harbor capital of the island and its main city, Charlotte Amalie, for a night on the town. The cook assigned to the detachment asked if he could hitch a ride. They were surprised by the request because this particular man never said a word to anyone. He was shy, if not stoic, and nothing, nothing ever seemed to raise his interest or anger or voice.

Shortly after they started the drive down the mountain, it started raining. The wind blew wildly. Trees swayed, debris rolled across the road. Visibility extended just beyond the end of the truck's hood. Suddenly, my friend, the driver, lost control of the truck, and they began sliding down the road, sideways, the driver's wheel spinning out of control, a crash imminent. My two friends screamed a mix of four-letter Anglo-Saxon and Germanic words, mostly f-bombs. The cook woke up from his torpid state and joined in. But he didn't scream anything recognizable. A lifetime of mostly non-vocal responses had left him ill prepared for responding vocally to a disaster. All he could scream was: "Hoo, hoo, hoo, hoo, hoo, hoo!" His dying words were going to be nothing more memorable than a string of incoherent sounds rhyming with "boo."

My friend regained control of the vehicle and they made it safely to town. The cook, having said nothing since his last "hoo," simply nodded his appreciation, opened the truck door, and slipped away into the night.

I never understood how a man, even a man of few words, facing imminent death could not come up with a better set of last words than "hoo." That is, until I faced the semis.

"Whoa, whoa, whoa, whoa, whoa," I screamed as the two semis headed straight for us. I slowed up and pulled into the soft shoulder, dirt and rocks splaying around us. Arlene screamed. This, too, shall pass, I hoped, and they did, right by us as if we were sitting in an invisible car. I pulled our car back onto the highway and drove on, determined more than ever to survive.

We turned off the highway from Celaya and entered our neighborhood, a few blocks from home. Still rattled from nearly becoming part of a truck's grill, I hit a *tope* too fast and heard the sound of something being removed, jerked away, untimely ripped, as it were, from my car. I pulled over, looked under the car, and grabbed the shield that since the day the car rolled off the assembly line had protected its undercarriage from damage and now hung precariously by a single thread. I tugged and it was a shield no more. I hurled the twisted, beat-up metal scrap into the back seat and drove home, bouncing over the few remaining *topes*, trailing clouds of exhaust, in a once-proud Audi Quattro that now looked and sounded like one of the town's downtrodden dogs.

When we stayed in our house, equipped with a land-line telephone and mobile phones, microwave, high-speed Internet, basic cable, and a subscription to Netflix, it was easy to forget where we were living. But once we ventured out onto the highways, I was reminded that Mexico, for all its recent advances and promise, remained a developing country with a lot of wild and crazy drivers.

Nonetheless, I was grateful that driving in Mexico enabled me to relive a treasured childhood memory, for every time I got behind the wheel and eased into traffic, I felt seven years old again, riding the bouncy metal car in Mr. Toad's Wild Ride at Disneyland, blasting through the library wall and entering the dark tunnel where surprises lurked.

When Cars Have Nightmares

How I Learned to Stop Worrying and Love the Firecracker

 *In which I discuss the proper celebration of a religious or civic holiday in central Mexico and why earplugs can be your best friend*

The bombing of San Miguel de Allende, Mexico, began shortly before sunrise on December 12. I was still in bed and chose to ignore the initial blasts, thinking it might be neighborhood kids getting a jump on the Christmas holiday season. The noise would be over soon, I was convinced. This couldn't be a regular occurrence?

But by seven A.M., there had been no less than fifty detonations, some distant and some too close for comfort. I sucked it up and ventured out on our second floor terrace to get a first-hand look at the destruction, where I observed explosions followed by huge puffs of soil knocked out of the countryside. From seven A.M. to eight A.M., from nine to ten—loud, unnerving rockets attacked us nonstop. By noon, I wandered out to ask an expat neighbor what was going on, and he explained it was the Feast of the Virgin of Guadalupe, the much-revered patron saint of Mexico. "I see," I said. But I didn't really see as much as I heard.

As the story goes, a peasant named Juan Diego heard music on a hill outside of Mexico City. The music emanated from a woman surrounded by a blinding light. She introduced herself as the Virgin and told Juan Diego to tell the local bishop to build a church on that spot in her honor. The bishop did not rise to middle management without some level of competence and was not so easily taken in. He demanded proof. After Juan Diego received another visit from the mysterious woman, this time involving roses in winter, the bishop finally had his proof, and Our Lady had her church.

Some anthropologists consider the Virgin of Guadalupe as a crossover between native Indian and Catholic beliefs. She is, in a single vision, both the Earth Goddess of Aztec lore and the Virgin Mary of Roman Catholicism. That was then and this is now, and today the Virgin of Guadalupe is the patron saint of all of Mexico. Consequently, throughout Mexico on December 12 there is, and will always be, much noise, with the bonus that long into the wee hours of the night, young girls and women named Guadalupe will be honored, while the rest of us toss and turn in our sleep, steaming and grumbling away.

The bombing continued and then stopped suddenly around mid-afternoon. I thought perhaps it was over. I told Arlene the worst had passed.

Two hours later the bombing picked up where it had left off. I had forgotten about *la comida*, the largest meal of the day normally consumed between two and four each afternoon. Even a full-range assault apparently took time off for a mid-day meal, a beer or two, an errand, and, time permitting, a brief siesta before restarting the celebration engine.

The explosions picked up volume shortly after sundown. They continued with increased ferocity throughout the early evening, and then pushed well into the night. I was told that much of the noise was designed to remind local parishioners to get their sinful bodies to church. If that's true, and if cherry bombs have replaced church bells, then religious attendance in Mexico was in worse shape than any of us thought.

After consulting a guidebook about San Miguel, however, I learned that the town is a festival town unlike most others, even by Mexican standards. At some point, San Miguel was recognizing and celebrating so many saints the central government told civic leaders to pick a few patron saints and make do with them. A quick glance at the calendar of events for a typical year in San Miguel reinforces the common belief that this town does, indeed, know how to punch a *piñata*.

January here begins, like much of the rest of the world, with a celebration on New Year's Day. On the sixth of January, all of Mexico celebrates Three King's Day, known as the Day of Epiphany in many other Christian countries. On this day the children of Mexico receive most of their holiday gifts. On the 17th of the month, St. Anthony's Day, all manner of animals from dogs to donkeys and parrots to chickens are brought to neighborhood churches to receive a priest's annual blessing. January 21 marks a huge celebration in San Miguel, complete with parades and firecrackers, for it's the birthday of General Ignacio Allende, the "Allende" in San Miguel de Allende.

To provide the appropriate book-end structure, *Sanmiguelenses* also celebrate his death later in the year. Between those two dates it's likely other Allende moments are celebrated, from the last time the general rode a horse to the first time he had a molar extracted. On the 24th, there is a celebration of religious pilgrims, not to be confused with the stateside homage to pilgrims eat-a-thon that takes place every November.

February is an average fiesta month, beginning with *Candelaria*, a day that marks the beginning of spring and the planting season with the sale of seeds and plants at a central location in town. Then there's Constitution Day, Valentine's Day, Flag Day, and, of course, Ash Wednesday, the official kickoff to the Easter season.

March and April can be lumped together because the Easter celebrations tend to fall within these months, and Easter in Mexico is one huge, long, non-stop treadmill of a holiday. But before I summarize the Easter festivities, also known as *Semana Santa* or Holy Week, I would like to squeeze in a few other holidays. The Feast of Our Lord of the Conquest occurs on the first Friday in March and includes indigenous tribal dances. On the 21st, the town celebrates the birthday of Benito Juarez. There's also the Day of the Divine Prisoner (*El Día del Divino Preso*), not quite the same as the Man in the Iron Mask but romantic nonetheless, and, of course, St. Patrick's Day, just another reason for another round of *cervesas, por favor*. On Friday of Sadness (*Viernes de Dolores*) the townspeople create altars in front of their homes. Strangers stroll by the altars and are fed by the homeowners, who give out everything from tamales to ice cream.

The Mexican Easter celebrations are many and moveable: Two Sundays before Easter, Friday before Holy Week, Palm Sunday (high point of the Catholic year), Thursday of Holy Week, Friday of Holy Week, Sunday of Holy Week (Easter). All in all, several reenactments and many salvos of fireworks occur, but my favorite is the afternoon of the Exploding Judases, an event that sounds like the name of a 1980s punk band from the East Village. Life-size, colorful mannequins, aka the "Judases," are suspended above a street, dangling from rope strung from the top of one building to a high point in one of the plazas. A Judas mannequin can be male or female, and quite often is made to resemble a national politician. More importantly, they are all wired with explosives, with a ring around the waist that spins the Judas when first ignited, and a larger bomb strapped just below the head providing the *coup de grâce*. Once the ring around the waist is lit, the mannequin twists and turns and sputters as the audience screams below it. Fireworks snap, crackle and, yes, pop. There's usually a slight pause before the final bomb goes off, which, did I already mention, is very loud and is accompanied by gleeful shouts from the crowd.

The powerful final blast separates the body from the head. When the smoke clears, all that's left is the statue's head, wearing a shocked expression and way too much makeup. The exact process is repeated until all of the mannequins have met their maker. A typical Exploding Judases event involves five rows of five mannequins, or twenty-five explosions, with one Judas at a time going up in smoke. Noise, thy name is Mexico.

May, June, and July are considered the hottest months, yet mere 100-degree weather is no obstacle to a fiesta.

Labor Day occurs on May 1, of course, and is followed three days later by the Feast of Santa Cruz, also known as the Day of Masons and Builders. That leads us to Cinco de Mayo, or the Anniversary of the Battle of Puebla, during which a vastly outnumbered force of Mexicans defeated a larger and better disciplined professional French army, even though the latter had the better chefs. Cinco de Mayo, celebrated partly in Mexico and mostly in the United States, involves tons of guacamole and the consumption of vast amounts of two-for-one margaritas.

Both the American version of Mother's Day and a Mexican version are commemorated, each on different days. In what some might see as a perverse joke, on Mother's Day in San Miguel children are given the day off from school, allowing them to spend more time at home, with mom doing the babysitting. May also gives us the Day of San Isidro (Patron of Rain & Agriculture), Ascension Day, and the Fiesta at *Valle del Maíz* (clocking in at around 96 hours of nearly non-stop fireworks).

June introduces Corpus Christi Day (Procession of the Blessed Sacrament), the Feast of San Antonio, and the Parade of Locos (*Dia de los Locos*). The Locos, aka Crazies, celebration is a kooky rite of early summer and one of my favorite fiestas. Entire neighborhoods, families, and businesses create floats or form bands or play dress-up, *en masse*, in anything from women's clothing to huge *papier-mâché* replicas of politicians' heads, and then march up and down streets. In the Mardi Gras tradition, those in the parade throw candy to the onlookers, packed three-four-five deep.

July is fairly quiet with only the Feast at Atotonilco, Feast of the Virgin del Carmen, and the Anniversary of the Death of Father Hidalgo to celebrate. And as far as I can tell, other than one of Latin America's most popular chamber music festivals, nothing much goes on in San Miguel during August, which is true for just about everywhere in the Northern Hemisphere as well. August, then, is generally considered a good time to get some sleep, as well as stock up on your supply of firecrackers for the next fiesta.

Which begs the question: Where do they buy these bombs? There was no obvious source. Unlike in the States, where in late June through early July in almost any part of the country you can stop by a small, temporary fireworks shed on your way home from work and pick up, say, a Roman candle or a box of sparklers from some guy named Skeets, who's missing two fingers. Yet in all of San Miguel there were no fireworks stalls, warehouses full of explosives, or basic armories where one might purchase noise makers *du jour*. It's one of the great mysteries of living in Mexico, and one I suspect I'll never solve.

And that leads us to September, a busy month to be sure. There's the annual President's State of the Union Address, akin to a big snoozefest, as it usually is elsewhere in the world, no matter which country or president, to open the month. By mid-month things start cranking up again. On the 13th of September they celebrate the Death of Child Heroes. Their Independence Day is honored over the 15th and 16th of the month, with *El Grito* (the Cry for Independence, not that stuff between your teeth), relentless fireworks, dances, and speeches, framed with many drinks. Sometime late in September, until recently the town held *Sanmiguelada*, its own version of the running of the bulls. It's been compared to spring break in Cancun but with more alcohol and mad bulls instead of college co-eds running around in wet T-shirts. Young men wearing white T-shirts and red bandanas flocked to San Miguel from all over Mexico to allow themselves to be chased by angry bulls around several narrow streets, with thousands cheering them on. The day before there was typically a running of the expats out of the city to safer towns nearby. However, catering to the whims and fears of the over thirty crowd, and perhaps to common sense, town officials have since abandoned *Sanmiguelada*.

Still in September, the 29th marks St. Michael's (the "San Miguel" in San Miguel de Allende) Day, although the actual celebration date can float from year to year. The birthday celebration is called *Alborada*, and it's an all-night festival that begins on Friday evening with fireworks and continues until 4 A.M. Saturday, concluding with a reenactment of the fire and brimstone battle between Lucifer and Saint Michael. This is the greatest religious celebration in the city, and when the battle is over, precisely at 5 A.M., the crowd sings "Happy Birthday" to St. Michael. Later on that same Saturday, there's a floral parade, and on Sunday a parade of indigenous tribes dancing in native costume.

September's celebrations cascade into October, which honors only two other holidays worth mentioning: the Feast of San Francisco on October 10 and Columbus Day on October 12. There's some party movement around the end of the month, with children celebrating an Americanized version of Halloween. But the next big events take place in November, opening with All Saints Day, followed immediately by Mexico's world-famous Day of the Dead (*Día de los Muertos*). Families take food and drink to burial plots, where they celebrate with deceased relatives and bring the dead up to speed on events of the year. Skulls and skeletons, whether as paper cutouts or sugar-coated candies, are everywhere. In homes and at public sites, commemorative altars or shrines to a loved one include candles, incense, chocolate candy, a six-pack of the deceased's favorite beer, along with a pack of his or her preferred smokes, all in case the deceased, as expected, stops by for a visit to see what's going on with the rest of the family. Later in November there's Mailman's Day and the Anniversary of the Revolution of 1910, both quite tame in comparison.

And we're back to where we started: December 12, and the Feast of the Virgin of Guadalupe. Cue the noise please, *maestro*. From December 16th through the 24th, *Las Posadas* occur, nine nights of candlelight processions during which Mexicans reenact the story of the Holy Family asking and being turned down multiple times for a room at a B&B, proving once again the strategic marketing value of Hotels.com. The *posadas* end on Christmas Eve, which leads to Christmas Day, with midnight suppers and church services to follow on December 31.

That brings us to January 1, as good a place as any to start anew. We repeat the above, shake well, and let stand.

Learning about these fiestas and festivals helped me to understand why the Mexican people remained warm, friendly, and downright happy, in spite of their daily struggle to make ends meet. They knew they were always just a day or two away from their next party. Don't get me wrong. When they can find work, they work very hard. But I suspect they party even harder. We observed pre-Hispanic and Hispanic celebrations, civic and religious holidays, fiestas marking an important day in the Mexican fight for independence or their civil war, and, of course, a never-ending supply of *quincineras*, mother-in-law birthdays, weddings, baptisms, and graduations. These were all celebrations worth hooting and hollering about.

"It's a good thing Mexico doesn't own a nuclear weapon," I told Arlene once.

"Why's that?"

"Because I'm sure they'd detonate it just for the noise. And they'd probably set it off above a town plaza during a fiesta weekend for maximum impact."

Not to harm anyone, mind you, but solely for the sound it would make and to earn the dying appreciation of the crowd below. That's because in Mexico if it's worth celebrating, it's worth a lot of noise. And I could live with that, I really could. I just couldn't sleep through it, even with wax ear plugs.

**Why I Live in San Miguel:
Reason #3**

My Body is a Temple That's been Sacked

 *Concerning certain feeble attempts to regain control of my own body in Mexico and do something meaningful about my abs*

I've always admired those tall and slender athletes with the perfect bodies, the long distance runners who have that lean and low cholesterol look. But I'm from the Endomorph tribe, and we're shaped more like bowling balls than bowling pins.

Like many lifelong butt-in-the-car, butt-in-front-of-a-computer types, I thought merely walking would be sufficient to reverse decades of inactivity and give me more of that snappy, thin-is-in look. But walking, however far or fast, even over cobblestones, even above the six thousand foot level, even in Mexico, wasn't going to do the trick alone. More drastic measures were needed. It was time for me to do something serious about my body, time to get off my size 36-wide and start exercising.

Back in the day I flirted with athleticism. I pumped iron, ran sprints, traversed obstacle courses, and played handball (as opposed to some wussy game with a racket). I wrestled on the varsity teams in high school and college. But as the decades passed, the only wrestling I was doing was with the television remote or my shoes.

Any display of strength was limited to opening a jar of mustard for Arlene. And flexibility had come to mean my willingness to eat chicken two nights in a row. Under such slothful conditions, exercising was not going to be easy.

So I joined a sports club. For all its differences, living in San Miguel was much like living in a town of comparable size in the United States. We even had our share of fancy sports gyms equipped with the latest equipment, including two-legged personal trainers. Arlene, to her everlasting credit, enrolled in a women's-only gym shortly after our arrival, where she began exercising three days a week. On two other days, she attended a yoga class. Before long her step was lighter and her smile brighter. Her clothes were hanging looser and no longer fitting.

My early days at a health club in San Miguel were spent competing with 80-year-old women for squatter's rights to one of three treadmills. Eventually I graduated to the "pit" and began pumping iron with the rest of the boys. Before long, my step was also lighter and my smile brighter; my clothes, on the other hand, still fit, which was probably the result of a diet that included fried pork rinds, Mexico's national snack and one of my favorite noshes. I thought of Curly, the cowpoke from the film *City Slickers*, who died because, as the Daniel Stern character said, he ate bacon with every meal. Fried pork rinds definitely had to go. The pork part might be okay; after all, it's the other white meat. But it was sandwiched between "fried" and "rinds," and that couldn't be good. I also slowed down on the drinking. I was fast on my way to reclaiming ownership of my own body.

And that's when the other Nike dropped.

Simply put, I wear the scarlet letter "H" on my chest for hypochondriac. Paying attention to the ups and downs of one's body isn't so bad, or at least it wasn't for me until the time I went to work in the medical library at a hospital. A hypochondriac working in the medical library is like a chocoholic working the graveyard shift at Hershey's or an alcoholic working at Jim Beam or a sexaholic cleaning pools at the Playboy Mansion or a shopaholic at Costco or a—I'm sure you get the picture. I was surrounded by opportunities.

Before long, every headache became a cerebral hemorrhage, every rash leprosy, every leg cramp the forerunner of an unidentifiable paralysis soon to make medical history and confine me to a wheelchair for the rest of my shortened life. The only good news, I thought, was they'd name the new disease after me. About the only conditions I couldn't get were denied me by my gender.

The library's manager, a woman, suffered severe menstrual cramps each month. Once when she was in pain and walked by my desk, I turned to a co-worker and said: "There but for the grace of a penis go I." The co-worker nodded without comment, for my dedication to illness was well known to the rest of the library staff. This particular co-worker knew that if I could get menstrual cramps, I would do so in a heartbeat. Or make that, in a premature ventricular contraction.

One night, a short few years after we were married, I was having breathing problems. I didn't want to wake up Arlene, even though I knew the end was near; instead, I wrote a description of my symptoms as well as instructions on what to do with my dead body, should I not make it through the night. In the morning, I went to work, my hastily improvised last will and testament note forgotten.

That evening Arlene confronted me with the evidence and waved the note in my face as sane person's Exhibit A. She said if I died, she would do whatever she wanted with my dead body, and at the moment she was inclined to ship my remains back to my parents via Bulk Rate mail.

In spite of all my imaginary health conditions, I did have one real, lifelong problem: the big wheeze—chronic asthma. I had hoped moving to the semi-arid central highlands of Mexico would eliminate my dependency on a daily inhaler. As a result, for the first six months I quit taking my asthma medication and felt wonderful for it. Then it caught up with me, and for several days I thought 800-pound gorillas were playing mumblety-peg on my chest. After that I took my daily inhaler and drank espresso three times a day to open my lungs.

While I was recovering from my asthmatic relapse, Arlene suggested I join her in a Tuesday-Thursday morning yoga class.

"It's very gentle. Nothing stressful about it."

"You know what happened the last time I took yoga."

"It wasn't yoga's fault. You're too competitive, that's the problem."

She was right. The last time I took yoga I lacked the proper attitude. My yoga outfit consisted of an Oakland Raiders T-shirt, a Saturday Night Live ball cap, and generic gray sweats. To make matters worse, the class was too New Agey for my tastes, especially when we were asked to visualize while doing the Tree Pose. I told the instructor I visualized a big bear on the ridge across from my "tree" and I was going to kill the beast, which promptly killed the more pacifist-minded instructor's use of the visualization technique. Then there were the poses themselves: cat stretch, downward facing dog, one-legged blind pigeon with shingles.

"It did help my breathing," I conceded.

"I'm telling you, you won't believe how easy this class is."

"Only one problem," I said.

"Oh?"

"Do I drink my espresso before I go to yoga or after? If I drink it before, then the yoga will reverse the espresso's adrenaline-like effects; if I drink it after, then the espresso will wipe out the calming effects of the yoga."

Arlene shot me a look. "You're smart. You'll figure something out," she said. "Are we still on for Thursday?"

It sounded like my kind of yoga, one with very low expectations and an even lower pulse rate. In fact, it almost sounded as if you could gently pass away during class on Tuesday and nobody would notice until they arrived for Thursday's class, surprised and impressed to see you maintaining the same stiff pose over 48 hours.

"I'm in," I said.

On Thursday morning, we walked through the yoga class door.

"Don't forget to turn off your cell phone," Arlene said. "The first time I was here some guy's cell went off in the middle of a pose. Everyone yelled at him, including the instructor."

"What was his punishment, seven years of bad karma?" I said.

"Don't laugh. The guy's never been back," she said.

"Was he banned for life? Oh, wait. Let me guess. He must have been banned for after life." Arlene frowned.

I checked my pants pockets, turned to my wife and smiled.

"No phone. I think I left it at home, recharging."

"So's mine."

"Let's just hope the President doesn't call."

We removed our shoes, inhaled enough incense to choke an Abyssinian warlord, and picked a spot for our yoga mats. I set my backpack next to my mat, removed my hat, jeans, and sweater, put them inside the backpack, and started stretching in my shorts. Arlene stared at me.

"Don't you have sweats or tights?" she asked.

"Couldn't find them," I said.

"That shirt looks a little snug. You're supposed to wear loose-fitting clothes."

"It's loose," I said. "See," I tugged at the sides.

"Well, remember, don't push yourself. You've been sick. It's yoga, not basketball."

"Don't worry. I plan on taking it easy."

Arlene was right. The class was an easy snore and didn't involve any of those body-twisting poses named after lower-order animals. Midway through the class I was breathing better already. Here's my ticket out of Asthmaland, I told myself.

Toward the end of the one-hour class, we were asked to place our bodies near a wall, lie on our backs, our arms by our side, and our knees bent to our chests. We were moving into the classic shoulder-stand pose, and would be allowed to lean against a wall to ease the pain. We then raised our feet to the ceiling. With just my head and shoulders on the floor, I wedged my hands under my lower back for support. My butt was tight against the wall, and my legs were shooting upward parallel to the wall. I found it hard to breathe either rhythmically or slowly, even at all. My stomach was in the way, and had it been detachable, I would have removed it. Making matters worse, my loose shirt was no longer just loose. It fell over my head, putting the squeeze on my throat, slowly garroting me as sure as any professional hit job. If I didn't escape the grip of my shirt, I would soon be sleeping with Luca Brazi and the fishes.

But I had other worries. The fatal flaw of not wearing tights became apparent when the wide legs of my shorts fell, bunching up near my crotch. I forgot about supporting my lower back and, instead, extended one hand to grab their loose fabric, holding it together as best I could. My other hand tugged at the collar of my shirt, trying to ensure a steady flow of air. It was all I could do to not make gagging sounds, hardly conducive to a true meditative state. At the same time, blood rushed to my upside-down head like midnight shoppers on Black Friday.

The nice instructor kept encouraging us, in her non-threatening monotone, to breathe in slowly from low in the stomach and count to five, hold our breaths for another count of five before exhaling—and to do it all through the nostrils. So much for the relaxing effects of yoga. My breathing was spasmodic. My stomach ached. My face was beet red. It was increasingly possible the last word I'd hear in yoga class that morning would not be "Omm" but some paramedic shouting "Clear" in Spanish. The shoulder-stand pose was taking forever, and I thought my day couldn't get any worse.

That's when my stomach released its first gurgle and I realized how bad things could really get. Oh, no, I thought, not loss of body control in public, not now, not in a small, poorly ventilated warm enclosure with everyone striving to reach a higher level of consciousness. San Miguel is a small town. We'd have to move. I shouldn't have had so much coffee before class, not to mention those cookies. I am, indeed, stupid, I told myself. Another gurgle, louder this time, followed by still another. All right, I said, I need to concentrate on my body. My body is a temple, and I am the high priest. You will behave and obey me, I told my body. You will not do anything to embarrass me. I am in control. I am the master. And to my surprise, the mantra worked; the gurgling stopped, my breathing improved, my body relaxed. I was on my way to that elusive higher plane.

Just then, a familiar sound ripped apart the silence in the room. It was the "Flight of the Bumble Bee" coming from my backpack. My cell phone was ringing. Snapped back to Earth, I scrambled to turn the phone off. I looked over to see if anyone had noticed. Who knew a higher consciousness could result in such dirty looks? My stomach gurgled back. Embarrassed, I apologized for my phone, grabbed my things, and fled the scene, seeking refuge in a coffee shop men's room.

Proposed SMA Summer Olympics Event #13

Nobody Knows the Spanish I Speak

 Concerning the difference between perro and pero, how we almost unintentionally bought our housekeepers a house, and why a huevo isn't just a huevo

It's not easy being a smart ass in a foreign language.

Case in point: We were dining in a popular restaurant in San Miguel. The menu included Aztec soup (*Sopa Azteca*), which, in Mexico, was like saying the menu included bottled water. Aztec soup was something of a restaurant staple in the country, a tomato-based yet spicy chicken soup garnished with avocado, sour cream, grated cheese, and tortilla strips. Although it was strong enough to hold its own as an entrée, it was often served as an early course.

"I think I'll order the Aztec soup," I told Arlene.

"You're ordering soup?" she replied. My comment had surprised her because she's convinced I have the appetite of a Sumo wrestler with two stomachs. I eat as if I'm trying to make up for meals I may, just may, have missed in a former life. Not only that, but when ordering in a restaurant I always go for the big protein dishes, hearty and manly fare. In a word, I eat large, and soup was simply not big enough.

"Not exactly. Hear me out."

"Oh?"

"I'll order the Aztec soup and when the waiter brings it and says 'Buen provecho,' I'll stare at the soup for a few minutes. Then I'll take one sip and wave him back over. He'll return to our table and ask, in his concerned Spanish, what's wrong?"

"Don't you dare" Arlene said.

"Then I'll tell the waiter, this is not Aztec soup, this is Mayan."

"Oy," Arlene sighed.

My wife took a sip from her bottled water and looked at me.

"You and your stupid word play. You really think he'll get it?" Arlene asked.

Of course he wouldn't get it, and therein was my problem. He would fail to understand that I was, as we like to say in the smart-ass biz, just cracking a joke, and a lame one at that. It's bad enough to explain your jokes in your native tongue; the prospect of trying to do so in a foreign language can cause cardiac arrest in an Olympian.

Besides, the waiters in San Miguel were extremely polite, so I doubt he would have even protested much. He would have apologized, looked hurt, and removed the soup to the kitchen while mumbling under his breath, in Spanish, the words "brain dead" and "gringos."

"No." I said. "I'd stop him before he took my soup away."

"What good would that do?"

"I'd tell him I was only kidding," I said.

"Okay, Mr. Funnyman. What's the Spanish word for 'kidding'?"

She had me there. The word was easily understood in English, yet it was very likely the innocent nature of the word would be lost in translation. I might unknowingly call him a baby goat in front of his co-workers, which could lead to an ugly scene involving thrown plates, glasses, and the local police. Even my laughing, designed to put him at ease, could be misconstrued as my laughing *at* him and not *with* him.

"I think I could pull it off," I said.

"Here's what you'd pull off," Arlene said. "The waiter would grab the bowl to remove it. You'd grab it back. You and the waiter would tug back and forth until the soup bowl would fly out of your hands and land upside down in my lap, ruining our dinner and my outfit."

When the waiter checked in with us later to see if we were enjoying our *comida*, I said I was. But here's how it actually went down:

Waiter: *Todo esta bien?*

Me: *Si. Mucho gusto.*

The waiter shot me a puzzled look. After a brief pause, he responded in English, having picked up on my unfamiliarity with his native tongue.

Waiter: I am very pleased to meet you, too.

He turned and walked back to the kitchen area, where after a few seconds we heard much laughter from the hired help. (Thank you, thank you, thank you. I'm here all week.)

Now you might think saying *mucho* would mean *a lot* and saying *gusto* would sort of mean *like* or, perhaps, might even have something to do with eating, with its gustatory connection. But no. *Mucho gusto*, as it turns out, is what you say when you meet or are introduced to someone, as in "I am pleased to meet you." I've often been accused of not knowing what I am talking about, but when it comes to Spanish, I really don't know what I'm talking about. I admit it. Nobody knows the Spanish I speak, not even me.

As always, Arlene was right. Smart-ass routines were not going to cut it in Mexico. Obviously, I wouldn't be ordering Aztec soup that night or anytime soon, unless I was ordering it to eat and not as a prop.

Moving to Mexico may have put a damper on being a smart ass, but in our local neighborhood I was considered something of a dumb ass, and rightly so. We lived in a traditional and somewhat self-contained Mexican middleclass neighborhood and had access to several *tiendas* or small mom and pop grocery stores, three *cocinars* (small diners out of one's home), a full restaurant, a holistic vet, three medical labs, one dentist, and half-a-dozen car repair shops. The largest of the small *tiendas*, Tony's, was a mere four doors down from our house, making it convenient and the destination of my first solo trip to the store.

The day after we arrived, I went to Tony's to pick up a few basics: milk, eggs, bread, the usual suspects. I grabbed the milk and bread but couldn't find the eggs, so I went to the check-out counter and nodded to the young man working there. I dusted off my high-school Spanish and asked, in my best broken-lingo, if he had any eggs? Using the words *tu* (for you), *tiene* (for have), and *huevos* (for eggs), I stated my case and smiled as I looked directly into his astonished eyes. The young woman standing next to him, a co-worker, looked up at her friend and giggled, then walked away to laugh loudly in the back room with unrestrained glee. After a polite pause the young man asked me how many eggs I wanted, went to the storage room, and returned moments later with my requested eggs twisted in a small see-through plastic bag. I thanked him and went on my way.

My mistake in syntax was only later explained to me, thanks to a bi-lingual friend. I had not asked the male clerk if he had any eggs. Instead, I had asked if I could have his private body parts. *Huevos*, as it turns out, is one of those tricky words in Spanish that can swing two ways, and one of those ways can get you in trouble.

I continued to speak the native tongue, when possible, and the first Spanish expression out of my mouth was always the easiest. I could give the standard "*buenos dias-tardes-noches*" greetings, give exact change, understand the time of day or make a general comment about the weather (*mucha lluvia* for much rain, for example). But as soon as the Spanish speaker continued the conversation or, worse still, asked me a question, rattling off a paragraph or two of words running so fast by me they tripped over each other, I was lost. In most cases, I'd smile and nod, agreeing to only God knew what.

Before leaving for Mexico, we received advice or inquiries on any number of topics from friends and co-workers. The most consistently asked question was about our fluency in the language, implying that if we could not speak the lingo, maybe we should reconsider moving there. After about the fifth time I was asked if I could speak Spanish, I found my way out of the loop. I said I had memorized three Spanish expressions that I thought would be sufficient: *Lo siento; Disculpame; Perdoname*. All were ways of saying, "I'm sorry."

In fact, I had memorized three expressions, which I hoped would provide me with ample cover in most situations: *No entiendo* (I don't understand); *No lo se* (I don't know); and *Que lastima!* (What a pity!). Not willing to let well enough alone, though, I would sometimes explain to these friends: "You realize, of course, *perro* means dog and *pero* means but, so if you run them together as *Perro Pero* you end up calling someone Dog Butt."

At some point I'd follow up my smart ass remarks with the truth: I took one year of Spanish in high school, more than forty years ago. As proof I'd recite an opening bit of conversation from one of the language tapes, permanently cemented to the lower benches of my mind:

"*Hola Isabel! Como estás?*"
"*Muy bien, gracias. Usted?*"
"*Muy bien. Donde esta la biblioteca?*"

Yes, I am not fluent in Spanish, to my everlasting shame; however, I would add proudly, if our car breaks down in the middle of Mexico, I could ask for directions to the nearest library and hope it has a mechanic on staff.

Linguistic hiccups notwithstanding, we moved to Mexico. And onward we slogged, slouching towards comprehension.

Then, one day I came home just as Arlene was explaining in Spanish to our housekeepers, Ana and Maria, that we were moving the following week to a new house one street over. It was hard to believe, but Arlene's Spanish was even worse than mine. I was a block ahead of her and three miles behind everyone else. But I was proud of Arlene, for she seemed to have cobbled together the right words: *nuevo casa, para usted, próxima semana*. She'd retrieved the words from the Internet minutes earlier, at one of those English-to-Spanish sites.

Unfortunately, the correct words were pieced together in the manner of a Chinese Crested, a goulash of good intentions but scary when put together as a whole. When she finished, our two housekeepers jumped up and cried. They hugged us and cried some more. Arlene asked what she had just said. I told her I believed she said we'd just bought them a new house and they could move in the following week. Arlene looked at their happy faces. Then she jumped up and cried. For the first time in my life, I regretted not taking that second year of high school Spanish.

We didn't buy them a new house, as it turned out. But they were okay with that because, when they'd seen the packing boxes, they had assumed we were moving back to the States. Instead they found out we were moving one street over and would be retaining their services.

Obviously, it was time for us to enroll in a language class. We asked around, read what others had to say about the language classes in town, and researched our options. Before long, we had registered for Level 1 Spanish at what many considered the most successful—and most expensive—language school in town.

We were the best students imaginable during our first week. We set our alarm and arrived early each day. We listened closely, did all the exercises, and finished our homework. We worked ahead and practiced constantly, challenging each other with the index cards. We even listened to the audio tape, throwing core verbs at each other like brats hurling water balloons.

During the second week, our enthusiasm and commitment waned. We still set the alarm clock and made it to class on time. We finished half of our homework assignments, almost. Outside of the classroom, we rarely talked about the class or the lessons, opting instead to act like students on summer break.

Our final week of class was a disaster. We no longer set the alarm clock and found ourselves rushing to class, totally unprepared and uninspired. We faked listening, even faked our exercises, and counted the minutes until class was over.

Not long after the class ended, our Spanish power verbs started to lose their potency. We were falling back into a reliance on English spiced with the occasional and wayward bit of Spanish. We avoided talking about the language program and how we had failed to follow up on the lessons or use whatever language skills we had learned. The problem wasn't the program, perhaps regarded as the best in town. It was us. Speaking for myself, I had neither the brain power nor the will power, not to mention I lacked the patience, to continue on to levels two and three of Spanish. I admired those expats who did. But I was too lazy. It seemed to make more sense to hire a bi-lingual Mexican to shadow me around town and pop out and translate whenever I needed him. We could become local superheroes: Expat Man and his loyal sidekick Berlitz. Better still, since it was my superhero story, I could be followed around town by a perky twenty-something female named Rosetta.

One day, months after the class, we were sitting outside in our courtyard sipping a drink and thumbing our respective ways through wordy American magazines, *Vanity Fair* and *The New Yorker*, all printed in comfortable, easy-to-understand English. I felt it was time to bring up the topic that dare not speak its name.

"Remember when we enrolled Cassie in that dog training class back in Portland?" I asked Arlene.

"Yes, of course," she said

"Halfway through the class we quit going. Remember? Cassie was too bored, so we said she challenged the class and passed it."

"I remember. Not the brightest move. But in our defense the class was at night during the work week, in another city, and our jobs were taking a lot out of us."

"That's not what I was getting at."

"Oh?"

What I was getting at was months later we had realized our mistake in dropping out of the class prematurely. The class wasn't for Cassie. It was for us. From that point on, we lost control over her. She owned us, rather than the other way around.

"We should have continued with the Spanish lessons," I said.

"Okay," said Arlene.

We paused and stared at each other, waiting for a trite light bulb to appear over one head or the other. It was a long wait.

"Should we sign up for section two of the class?" I asked, breaking the silence.

Arlene shook her head.

"Too expensive. We'll just fall into the same trap and stop going. How about buying a language tape? We can listen to it on our own terms," she said.

Now I shook my head. "We'll never listen to it."

"You're right. Immersion?" she asked.

"What?"

"You know, we move in with a Mexican family and immerse ourselves in the language. This town offers several great immersion programs."

"What about Cassie and Sadie?"

We both shook our heads. The more we thought about our dog and cat and the prospect of taking them into a happy Mexican family, the more vigorously we shook our heads.

"Besides, we already have a house," Arlene said.

"We'd probably corrupt the family anyway. They'd end up cursing in English like a sailor on shore leave and dropping in bits of Yiddish," I added.

We stared at each other, looked around the room, continued to wait for inspiration to strike. And, you know, it did. Eventually. It always does, even if the light bulb that goes off over one's head is the older and inefficient incandescent model.

"Let's hire a tutor, one of the instructors from the class," Arlene suggested.

"A tutor's not in our budget," I said.

"Since when do you worry about the budget? Besides every year for the holidays we buy something for the house we're in and this year we'll buy something for us. We live in the house. We'll hire a tutor," she said, upbeat at the prospect.

"Deal," I said.

We shook on it. Giving each other a tutor for Christmas might not rival the Gift of the Magi, but at least it would be the gift that kept on giving. Over time, our limited Spanish would no longer be an impediment.

"We're never going to be fluent in Spanish. We're old dogs."

"Yep," I said. "No matter how many tutor visits we clock in, we won't be discussing the finer points of art history in Spanish with a local artist or engaging in theological discussions with a parish priest any time soon."

"At least I'll be able to talk with Maria and Ana," said Arlene.

"And I'll be able to buy eggs at Tony's without being publicly humiliated."

But when Christmas rolled around we found other gifts for each other, and our language acquisition skills continued to languish.

Alternative Use #8 for Nopals

Waiting for Audi

 *Regarding the events of the Week of the Dead, mysterious problems with our Audi, and the true meaning of Mañana*

In my time I've owned a Pinto, a Buick, and a Corvair, which sounds like the fleet Christopher Columbus would have taken to the New World had his trip been sponsored by Detroit instead of Spain. Over time, of course, several other makes and models earned parking spots in my personal fleet of automobiles, from classic Chevys and Fords to the upscale Audi we took with us to Mexico.

I received my first car as a gift from an uncle even before I was old enough to drive. The car was all that a teenager in the 1960s could hope for: a two-door 1955 Chevy. Every day after school, I'd sit in my car and spin the steering wheel, pretending to drive. I'd add cartoon-like sound effects and fantasize about "cruising Main" with my friends, looking cool, picking up chicks. I cleaned the inside and outside of that car more times a day than Howard Hughes scrubbed his hands.

Two months later, an adult cousin with a young family needed a car, so my parents, after duly running their decision by me, passed on to the cousin the car that an uncle had passed on to me. After all, we agreed I was a year away from having a license and would have plenty of time to find another car.

And sadly enough I did. Many of them.

In college I drove a metal-flake green Sunbeam Tiger, the brand of car Don "Maxwell Smart" Adams, Agent 86, tooled around in on the *Get Smart* television show. Later, I owned a pristine four-door one-owner, duo-tone 1957 Ford Fairlane, as well as a bright yellow Super Beetle that attracted bees as if it were a honeycomb on four wheels. There was the small Toyota truck that was a legend in its own time for the way it shimmied out of control whenever it carried anything larger than two bags of groceries in its bed. Then there was the four-door, dark "K" Chrysler that looked like it came straight from the DEA car pool. And a Ford Mustang that reeked of Crab *Cioppino* when the weather turned too hot or too cold, since we had spilled leftovers from a crab feed in the back of the car one weekend and could never get rid of the smell.

Arlene, as the majority of her dowry, brought an electric blue AMC Gremlin named Gregory into our marriage. I was convinced the car was possessed, something of an Amityville Horror of the highways.

The radio only worked when it was freezing outside. The passenger door never opened, no matter how many of us pulled. The entire top of the back seat collapsed if touched the wrong way. And the windshield wipers, in a failed attempt at solving the intermittent windshield wiper problem, were tied to a ritual that restricted their operation to whenever you let off the gas pedal, making any long-range drive in a thunderstorm difficult and twice as long as it should have been. When it was raining, I'd accelerate, then back off the gas pedal and wait for the windshield to clear before accelerating again. Sometimes this would go on for hours. Is it any wonder I'm neurotic?

Not many can say this—or would be willing to admit it—but we eventually bought a Yugo, which at the time was the cheapest new car in America and still overpriced. Our logic was flawless: we owned a business and needed to make trips around town, picking up and dropping off assignments, so why not get a car that was fuel efficient and cheap? Unfortunately, the best thing about buying a Yugo, as it turned out, was the T-shirt they gave each new owner. Bold letters on the front proclaimed: "Wherever I go, Yugo."

We named the car "Victor" for all the obvious literary reasons, and it turned out, indeed, to be *Le Miserable*. Anyone who owned a Yugo could have warned the world powers that the former country of Yugoslavia was bound to fail. The interior of our Yugo was a dizzy collection of browns, as if every art school in that troubled, fractionalized country had been asked to contribute a different shade. Then when art school administrators followed up to ask if the brown should be dark, light, tan, earthy, crusty, rusty, dusty, chocolate, taupe, beige, cream or whatever, the Yugo spokesman had replied in a stern, Slavic voice, "Brown is brown." I am here to tell you, brown is not brown. We had a full rainbow of browns, from the seats to the dashboard to the ceiling, floor mats to door handles, a crazy quilt of earth tones.

The Yugo's gear shift was so hard to move into the correct position that it took both of my hands and all of my strength to get the car into reverse. And I'm the guy who opens jars in our family! One time when I stopped for gas, the attendant asked for the gas cap key. I told him the car didn't have a locking gas cap. He returned minutes later to tell me he couldn't get the cap off without a key. I walked out and joined him, both of us pulling the cap, but with no luck. Finally, he grabbed an enormous jaws of life wrench, the ones used by emergency rescue personnel to extricate crash victims, and unscrewed the cap. As he explained to me, the gas tank had "vapor-sealed." He told me to never fill the tank and I wouldn't have any problems. Unfortunately, my gas gauge wasn't working, so that meant I could never fill the tank and, at the same time, I would never know how much gas I had in it. I was constantly driving into gas stations and getting three dollars worth of the stuff. As I said earlier, is it any wonder I'm neurotic?

In fairness, we all carry around such horror stories, for is there a car owner with soul so dead who never to himself hath said: "This car's a piece of crap!" Let's face it, at one time or another the black sheep in any family is a car.

Eventually, Arlene and I moved up through the ranks of the middle class and acquired two very reliable cars: a BMW and an Audi Quattro. We could take only one car with us to Mexico and the competition wasn't even close. The Audi won hands down. Winning, though, had nothing to do with a J.D. Powers or *Consumer Reports* rating or even an emotional attachment to one vehicle over the other. It had everything to do with our dog. Cassie hated the BMW, and the one and only time I could get her in that car I had to carry her in, despite her growling and snarling. The ultimate driving machine lost out to the whims of a dog.

Most likely, the Audi did prove to be the better choice. It had more room, was four-wheel-drive (just in case climate change were to introduce snow to semi-arid Mexico), and included a luggage rack on top. So what if a local gas station attendant predicted on the day we left Portland that the Audi probably wouldn't make it out of Oregon, let alone reach Mexico. It accomplished both feats, working like a champ. And it continued to work until we suffered what Arlene and I came to refer to as the Week of the Dead (*Semana de los Muertos*).

It was early May, on average the hottest month of the year in San Miguel, when we returned from a visit to the States. We always told ourselves our luggage would be lighter on the return trip, but it never was. This time, in addition to our clothes and pounds of books, we carried back with us heavy drapes. By the time we made it to Mexico, my right shoulder had given out from lugging the luggage. I had developed bursitis. My right arm was useless and would remain useless for several weeks, dangling by my side like a teenage groupie. That was the first death during our Week of the Dead.

The second death came around the same time and was an appropriate extension of the first. My laptop computer died, totally, irrevocably. We were able to retrieve the data, but, since I couldn't type even if I wanted to because of the pain in my right arm, it turned out to be as good a time as any to order a new computer.

The third death that week was our house. Or, more correctly, it was the death of the electrical power that came from the street and serviced our house. Although the dwelling was new, we quickly learned that new did not necessarily mean up to code, if there was such a thing. The house still relied on old fuse-box technology. Apparently, the power went from the service box, the facade, to the fuse box, the real power behind the curtain. And one day that week the fuse box blew up.

We hired an electrician to replace the fuses with a modern service box. While installing the new service panel, he also discovered that our house—the entire house, mind you—was not grounded, a startlingly fact since we were approaching the thunderstorm season and the odds of one of us ending up a crispy critter would be improved by such an omission.

However, the biggest death of all that week was our Audi, which was death number four, thus putting a wrench into my belief system that bad news and bad comedy come in threes. The car had been running rough for weeks, and even a trip to the Audi dealership in *Queretaro*, a city of three-quarters of a million residents and only a 45-minute drive away, did not resolve the problem. The dealership mechanic, very friendly and spiffy-looking in his Audi-logo splashed outfit, told us they didn't have the required part and wouldn't be able to get it. Instead of fixing our car, they washed it, which was very nice of them all things considered. But now the Audi seemed beyond hope. Minutes after I started it, the car would boil over, indicator lights would flash, oil drip. I asked around the neighborhood for a mechanic.

"Have you tried Jesús?" a neighbor suggested.

"I don't know him," I said.

"He's the guy who owns the car repair shop on the Ancha, near the bank."

"Oh, that Jesús."

"I trust him. He's proud of his work and takes his time."

"That's okay. There's no rush," I said, realizing I would regret the words "no rush" as soon as they left my mouth.

I passed by the shop every time I walked into town and didn't realize it was a working garage, since the cars parked in front of it were mostly covered in dust. Many were beat-up and ancient, with long bodies, big fins, low ceilings, frayed and hupcapless tires, bumpers held together by wire, doors held together by tape, a coat of paint that was mostly rust, and the occasional plastic sheet for a windshield. Hoods on half of the cars were up and yawning.

Almost anywhere in America, you would have been looking at the inventory of an automobile graveyard. But here, the cars were still on life support: Ford LTDs, Larks, Darts, Comets, Galaxies, a who's who or what's what from the Big Three up north, now destined to live out their days retired in sunny Mexico. The difference, of course, is that these babies were still working— Jesús made sure of that.

On Monday, I drove the Audi into the lot, parked it, asked for and found Jesús, a short and stocky man, unexpectedly neat, his blue shirt tucked into black pants. He looked at me suspiciously, which is probably how he thought I looked at him. Once we overcame our suspicions and he realized I was dropping off my car for some cash business, we both smiled. I explained in a mix of broken Spanish and English what I thought was wrong with the car. Simply put, it was overheating and burning oil (I could still hear that Portland mechanic's warning). I couldn't drive the car more than ten minutes without the radiator erupting in steam and the idiot lights going crazy. Jesús popped the hood, and three of his workers gathered around, peering in and talking in low, hushed voices as if they were hospital interns scrubbing for surgery and the patient was listening in. Jesús slammed down the hood, wiped his hands, then shook my hand and said: *"Mañana."*

I walked home and told Arlene the car would be ready tomorrow. The next day, I waited until after five in the afternoon before returning to pick up my car, making sure I gave them enough time to work on it and to have their *comida*. My Audi was in the same place I had left it and Jesús was nowhere to be found. I was told that he was in Celaya picking up car parts, and that I should return *mañana*.

The next day I walked over to the garage around ten in the morning, thinking I'd catch Jesús before he took off to another city. He was not in yet, but I was told he was due to show up around noon. I walked the ten blocks back home in the rising heat and waited until noon, returning to the garage under an even hotter sun. Jesús had not arrived but was expected *"un momento,"* a phrase, I was to sadly learn, that held the stretching capability of Spandex. After forty-five minutes of waiting momentarily, I returned home. Sometime after six in the early evening of that day, I returned to the garage, and this time I found Jesús, a minor victory to be sure but one that was short-lived. He hadn't had a chance to work on my car but told me to return *"mañana"* and it might be ready. I finally figured out that *mañana* is another rather amorphous term and hoped to pin him down by asking for an exact time *mañana* when I should drop by. *"Mas tarde, tres o quatro,"* Jesús said, which I correctly assumed to mean tomorrow afternoon, Thursday, between three and four. I nodded, we shook, I left, he returned to his office.

I told Arlene the car would be ready the next day, Thursday, in the afternoon. Now with a better understanding of how to gauge time, I showed up at Jesús' garage at four P.M., even though by nature I am an early person.

In Mexico you don't just barge in and demand to talk to someone about your car. You need to ease into the conversation, first greeting each other, then talking about the hot weather, and only after a few minutes, casually mentioning your car as if your whole point for being there was an afterthought. It's a polite and civilized way to do business, I admit. Jesús would always shake his head and tell me, *"Es muy difícil."* I would nod and say, *"Si."* He would then say, *"Mucho trabajo."* I would nod and say, *"Si."* Then if he needed more money up front for a particular part, this is the point at which he would hit me up for it. I, of course, would give him the money and say, *"Si."* And, of course, I would walk home. Twice a day, I'd walk over to the garage to pick up my car, and twice a day I'd walk home without it.

Late on Friday afternoon I stopped in and visited with Jesús and his workers, one of whom was sitting on the engine block inside of the open hood of a car and twisting pieces of metal with a wrench. I gave Jesús money to buy beer for the boys, thinking I'd grease the crankshaft a bit. From that point on, whenever his workers would see me they'd wave and shout, *"Hola, Amigo."* I was one of the boys.

But to no avail, for there my Audi still sat, unattended, unloved. I knew if they didn't work on the car by Saturday that the shop was closed on Sunday and the coming Monday was a fiesta, thus no work would be done until Tuesday at the earliest.

On Tuesday, Day Eight of captivity, my Audi still sat in Jesús' garage, looking sad and alone. Arlene and I rode by the garage in a bus and looked at our car, wistfully, as if we were displaced farmers looking at the old family homestead now in the hands of an impersonal bank. That afternoon, I returned to the garage and asked to see Jesús. He came out from his office, and we chatted about the weather. I asked about my car. Again, he said it was a very difficult problem to fix that would require a lot of work. Again, I nodded in agreement with his diagnosis. Again, he said, "*Mañana.*" Again, I walked home.

"No car? Arlene asked.

"No car," I said.

"How much is this going to cost?" she asked.

"I've a feeling with all of the money we're spending on the Audi, Jesús will either name his next son or a new wing of his garage after me."

"It'll get fixed, things always do," said Arlene, the eternal optimist.

"Our Audi will be speaking Spanish before we will—at least it will have more Mexican auto parts than German ones," I added.

"Will it be ready tomorrow?"

"Depends upon how you define tomorrow. I used to think *mañana* meant the day after today. Now I know what it really means: Not today."

On Wednesday, as we passed by the garage in a bus on its way into the center of town, Arlene and I caught our first glimmer of hope. Our Audi was in the "pit" of the garage, and someone was actually working on it. Later that afternoon, I walked back to the garage and met with Jesús. We chatted. He looked serious. I gave him more money for another part. And I walked home. *Mañana* couldn't get here soon enough.

Thursday morning, the tenth day without our car, and Jesús told me to return in the afternoon at two P.M., more or less. I did, and he took me for a glorious spin in my Audi, up the steep *Libramiento*, onto *Salida de Queretaro*, down several bumpy roads by where the huge open air market takes place on Tuesdays, and back to his garage. Jesús beamed, as if holding a new grandson. The thermostat held steady, locked in the preferred position halfway between hot and cold. The oil gauge did not climb. The car did not buck. Even the air conditioner worked again. My God, I thought, the man actually knew what he was doing.

Later, I would retell the story to my expat neighbor George, a man who was something of a skeptic about his new life in Mexico.

"Even the dealership mechanic in Queretaro couldn't fix the Audi and he had a lot of computer equipment," I bragged. "But this guy on the corner, this Jesús guy, got the job done the old fashioned way."

"Does he have a computer?" George asked.

"I don't know. But even if he does, it's probably an Atari. He just figured out what needed to be done and did it," I said.

"Maybe he just turned off all the warning signals," said George.

"What?" I asked, stunned.

"You know, maybe the indicators are shut off, so you won't know if it's overheating until it's too late."

"Hmm," I said, and walked away.

Now I'm pretty much a glass is half empty type, but even I had not considered that possibility. But if Jesús merely turned off warning lights to fool me, then he must have fooled the Audi, too, because the car ran like a charm from the day he fixed it, and for the rest of our stay in Mexico. I'd put my money on Jesús again anytime. He might not have the right equipment or the right parts, but he had the right stuff, and that was good enough for me, even if *mañana* is always more than a day away.

**Why I Live in San Miguel:
Reason #12**

We'll Always Have Parasites

 *In which I brag about having an iron gut and promptly offend the Stomach Gods, with appropriate punishment meted out in a retelling not for the squeamish*

During the summer months between my sixth and seventh grades, I read *How to Win Friends and Influence People*, *Think and Grow Rich*, *Let's Eat Right to Keep Fit*, and *The Iliad*. The international best-selling *Win Friends* seemed to be more about sucking up than being honest, which would eventually pay dividends when dealing with the nuns at my school. Unfortunately, thinking and growing rich never took hold on the slippery slope of my mind, then or now. I understood Homer's great work about the Trojan War only after buying and reading the *Classics Illustrated* ("Featuring Stories by the World's Greatest Authors") comic book version of the epic. These versions, I confess, helped me through more than one book report.

But Adele Davis' classic work on the connection between what you throw down your throat and how your body responds to it was a second Bible in our household. And I devoured her book, much like those famous tiger shakes she praised high and low. Suddenly that summer I added "lecithin" and "essential amino acids" to my vocabulary and to my diet. I had no choice, for at the time my father was a health nut, and the nut doesn't fall far from the tree.

For breakfast, I ate wheat germ as my dry cereal of choice while my friends ate Sugar Pops, now re-branded as the nutritionally more acceptable Corn Pops. Our freezer stored oranges and tangerines for Vitamin C. Our candy dish contained dried apricots for Vitamin A. We had unshelled peanuts and unsalted sunflower seeds around for whatever vitamins or nutrients they delivered. And there was always plenty of milk for the all-important Vitamin D, much needed since we were getting a mere 15 hours of bright sunshine daily in Sacramento during the summer. I would add a spoonful of brewer's yeast to my water, stir vigorously, and pretend I was drinking a milk shake. Fresh carrot juice was even better than a milk shake and I'd consume the juice every chance I'd get. My imagination rarely let me down.

Years later, when I was on the high school wrestling team and needed to "make weight" for an important tournament, I starved myself for two weeks, limiting myself to 500 calories a day. Because of my earlier interest in minerals, vitamins, and nutrients, I knew exactly what to do. I would supplement—more accurately, replace— my normal required caloric intake with the whole macrobiotic package. I would also eat high-in-iron liver at night, disgusting stuff which today I can't even look at without running the other way. Nonetheless, the night before the tournament I was still a pound and change too heavy.

Drastic measures were required. After my dinner of pan-fried liver, I broke off a small cube of the popular chocolate-flavored ex-lax® laxative, ingested it, and waited. Nothing happened. Another twenty minutes passed, and still no reaction. I broke up several cubes and chewed them all. I spent a good part of that night in the bathroom, a sad state of affairs for the rest of my family because our house was small and poorly ventilated. If my paternal grandfather, a retired railroad man, had been staying with us, he would have neatly recapped the situation with one of his favorite expressions: "Smells like something crawled up inside that boy and died."

No one died at our house that night, but I lost the weight I needed to lose. All day during the wrestling tournament, I consumed glasses of brewer's yeast, hoping that a sudden influx of so much vitamin B would restore my strength, replenish my system, make me stronger. I couldn't eat anything solid because I couldn't retain food; my body was like a Slip 'n Slide toy. Whenever my stomach gurgle-gurgle-gurgled, I knew I had less than thirty seconds to make it to the bathroom. At the end of one match, my opponent had me in what was called a tight waist grip, with one of his arms squeezing my stomach. With just seconds to go my stomach began to gurgle. I grabbed one of his fingers and bent it back. He yelled and let go of me, and the match ended. My coach walked over to congratulate me, but I flew by him like The Flash, barely making it to the locker room in time. Later that night I had to sleep sitting in a chair, for brewer's yeast billowed through my body. I had forgotten: yeast rises. My stomach was distended, and had someone stuck a pin in my side, I think I would have flown around the ceiling of our house until I ran out of air, like a deflated balloon.

Since those gurgling halcyon days, my stomach had been rock solid, in some regards the most dependable part of my body. As I mentioned before, Arlene loves to cook and I love to eat. There's very little on a menu I will not try, with the possible exceptions of creamed corn, eggplant, and, of course, liver.

While preparing to leave Portland for Mexico, we were warned by many friends about the food "down there." We were told countless times never to drink tap water (unless we're in New York City, we never do), stay away from salads, be careful about the meats, and so on. Forget about ice cubes in your drink and always use bottled water when brushing your teeth, they said. One seasoned traveler to Mexico warned us to stay away from the luscious-looking strawberries sold on the street because they were beautiful but deadly, like a *femme fatale* in a gumshoe novel. Our friends joked about singing in the shower, suggesting we duct tape our mouths shut. They offered more jokes about *Montezuma's Revenge*. We countered that the reverse was just as true for people coming from Mexico to the United States: they sometimes suffer what is known as *The Empire Strikes Back*. All of this advice was good, honest, well-intended. We assured everyone that we'd be on high alert and not to worry.

Once we arrived at our rental home, we began to hear stories—usually second-hand, from passing conversations with friends or mentioned in email strings—about six-inch worms suddenly appearing in bowel movements, Loch Ness Monsters of the toilet bowl. Or about the woman with four holes in her liver, all caused by undetected and unwelcome parasites. Or the man who was flat on his back for weeks, again thanks to parasites, and whose treatment took several months and who has still not fully recovered — and may never. But such stories remained in the realm of expat folklore because we were, personally, doing fine. We washed everything, drank bottled water, didn't sing in or out of the shower, and never considered buying food from a street vendor.

Then one day, while walking Cassie in the neighborhood, we met another couple, also Americans and also walking a dog. They looked to be in their late 30s, dressed casually in shorts and light tops, and friendly. The man smiled and extended his hand.

"Where're you from?" he asked.

"Portland, Oregon," I replied.

"Just visiting?"

"We've been living here since last December," Arlene said.

"We're from Wisconsin. Been here for three years now. Is that right, Hon?"

Hon smiled and nodded.

"Retired?"

"Gosh, no. I work at an industrial container company. We're based in Wisconsin, you know, but have a plant down here in Mexico, not far from San Miguel."

"You live here full-time then?" I asked.

"Yes, I guess. Every two months they send me back to the States for three weeks, you know. To visit the main plant and to be with my wife."

Arlene and I stared at the woman next to him.

"Where are my manners. This here's my wife, Bonnie. I'm Wayne. She decided to come down this time instead of me going up there. We do that sometimes."

We exchanged introductions.

"How do you like it down here?" I asked.

"Oh, gosh. It's different here, you know," said Wayne. "I can't speak the language. And I still can't handle the food, ever since my first day here."

"What do you mean the food?" asked Arlene, always probing for the latest foodie insider tips.

"First day on the job and it's three in the afternoon, you know, and my co-worker comes in. He says, 'What say we have a little lunch?' So, I say, 'You betcha.' So he takes me to this place over by the road to *Queretaro*. It's a chain called Coyotes."

"We know the place," I said.

"I'm trying to cut down, you know, because of my weight. Besides, I look around and I see stuff I've never seen before. So I play it safe, you know."

"Safe?"

"I order a salad."

"A salad!?" repeated Arlene.

"You got that right. One of those big dinner jobbies. With shrimp."

Again, in disbelief, Arlene repeated what he said: "Shrimp!?"

"Hmm," I said, sneaking a glance at her. Arlene was looking appalled.

"So, at the end of the meal I say, 'What's the damage?' and he says, 'My treat.' I thank him and then he shakes his head. We're walking out to the truck, don't cha know, and he says, 'I'm surprised you ordered it. There's only one thing you shouldn't order down here and that's the salad. And it's a good idea to stay away from the fish, especially the shrimp. This ain't Veracruz.' Heck of a note."

"Hmm," I nodded.

"You know, lotta guys would have warned you before you order and eat something you shouldn't order and eat. Heck of a note."

"Why didn't he warn you before you ordered?" I asked.

"That's what I said. 'Got to learn lessons for yourself down here,' this guy says to me. 'Only way to learn.' Did I get sick? You betcha. Flat on my back, don't cha know. I was married to the toilet, as they say, for a week or more. No offense, Hon."

"None taken, Hon," Bonnie said and smiled.

"Sicker than a dog I was. Sicker than a dog."

We all looked down at our dogs.

His dog looked up at him, then looked over at our dog, shook his head sadly, as if to say, "I told him to stay away from the lettuce. And shrimp in the desert? Don't get me started." And this from a four-legged creature that will eat anything thrown away in the bushes or left behind on the street.

We said goodbye and went our separate ways, ever more mindful of food vigilance. But, as I said, we were careful and remained healthy, with no signs of any gastrointestinal events. However, weeks later, we stopped in to visit our artist friend Pattie, an expat who lived in our neighborhood, and the kind of person who even in retirement was over-committed and somehow remained highly energetic. But this time, she looked tired, and we were worried about her.

"I have no energy. I think I finally caught a parasite. I'm hoping it's just *Giardia*," said Pattie.

"*Giardia*, what's that?" I asked.

"You've never heard of *Giardia*?" Arlene asked me. "It's a fairly common parasite, even in the States. I think you get it from water."

"Do you drink bottled water?" I asked.

"Bottled water can be worse for you than tap water," Patti said. "Studies have shown bottled water can contain traces of *E. coli*. Some bottled waters actually start as tap water. They're filtered before being bottled," said Patti. A political activist all her life, Patti kept up on all things current and was wary of American corporate involvement in Mexico or, for that matter, anywhere else in the world. "Coca-cola and Pepsi have a monopoly on the filtered water business down here," she summarized, as if that one sentence said it all.

"I guess the safest thing to drink is tequila," I said.

"Did you hear about the expat who had four holes eaten through his liver?" Pattie asked, ignoring my comment and only slightly changing the subject.

"We heard," Arlene said.

"Parasites," Pattie declared, nodding as if bowing to the inevitable.

Days later I bragged to Arlene about my iron stomach. I felt fine, I told her. Nothing seemed to bother my stomach, I said. Arlene reminded me that we were both very careful in what we ate and drank, and she, especially, took great pains to ensure our food was clean and safe. But it was too late, for in that brief bring-it-on moment I had angered the Gods of the Upper Abdomen, and in a matter of days I, suddenly enfeebled, was married to the toilet.

The next day we went to see Dr. Teresa, a woman fluent in Spanish, French, English, and, I was hoping, parasites. This was to be my second use of her healing skills. Earlier in the year, she'd fixed my bursitis problem with a series of Vitamin B12 injections, infused with a special anti inflammatory. After five consecutive days of injections, the pain left and never returned. Although trained as a conventional internist, Dr. Teresa distrusted modern pharmacology and preferred to treat her patients with natural remedies as a first course of action, when possible.

We didn't have medical coverage in Mexico for doctor visits, yet the cost for a visit was similar to what we'd paid in the States under our medical care plan as a co-pay, the equivalent of twenty-five U.S. dollars. Perhaps best of all, a visit to the doctor in San Miguel wasn't like speed dating. Dr. Teresa spent plenty of time with me, perhaps as long as thirty minutes each visit.

"What did you have to eat or drink that was different than normal?" Dr. Teresa asked.

That's when the Eureka light went on, and if I had been feeling better I would have jumped up. Instead, I turned to Arlene and smiled weakly.

"Carrot juice," I said.

"What?"

"When I was waiting for you to finish your ceramics class, I had a carrot juice from the school café."

"Why?"

"Why not? It was on the menu."

"There's a chance that's what caused your episode. Carrots

are hard to clean here, like strawberries. You might be lucky and only caught some bacteria and not any parasites," Dr. Teresa said.

"So, let me get this straight. I was done in by a healthy drink?"

"Possibly."

Who said irony was dead.

"The longer you live down here the more likely you'll catch a parasite or an amoeba, some kind of digestive problem," the doctor went on. "Eighty to ninety percent of the people here have amoebae in their systems."

I pictured tapeworms crawling inside me and holding a family reunion. I must have looked stricken, for she immediately smiled and tried to make me feel more at ease.

"Most amoebae are harmless, however," she said.

"That's good to know." I nodded and looked over at Arlene. She smiled and gave me one of her what'd-I-tell-you looks.

"Unfortunately, the most dangerous ones don't always show up in the lab tests. At least not in the early stages," she followed up.

I was back to feeling stricken. "What if it happens again?"

"You do what we all do. Watch what you eat and drink. Wash your fruits and vegetables in an iodine solution. Stay away from the street vendors. Wash your hands a lot. Don't touch your mouth after touching a doorknob or a window. I'd be very careful with pork, bacon, ham, hot dogs. Just follow the usual common sense rules of cleanliness and good hygiene."

Since common sense wasn't anything I was accustomed to following, I remained skeptical.

"That's it?" I asked.

The doctor opened her desk drawer and removed a pad of paper. "I'd like you to go over to the lab on Hildago and get tested," she said. "In the meantime, I'm giving you a prescription that should help. We'll know more later."

For over fifty years I've pretty much gone through life on autopilot, and it was finally catching up with me. I walked away amazed at how many ways there were to skin a mortal, and we were only in the amoebae section of the *Physician's Desk Reference*.

Later that evening, after taking Immodium D and popping a few Pepto-Bismol tablets, I ate a small portion of steak for the protein I thought my body lacked. Before the night was out, I was back inside the bathroom, shades of my high school years, listening to the sounds of my stomach gurgling like Mt. Etna, once again married to the loo. My mind wandered, and I imagined what would have happened if the film *Casablanca* had been set in San Miguel instead of Morocco.

Rick: If that plane—

Ilsa: Bus. San Miguel doesn't have an airport.

Rick: If that bus leaves the depot and you're not with him, you'll regret it. Maybe not today. Maybe not *mañana*, but soon and for the rest of your life.

Ilsa: But what about us?

Rick: We'll always have parasites. We didn't have, we, we lost them until we came to San Miguel. We, I, got them back last night. It must have been the strawberries. That's right, somebody took the strawberries. They must have had a duplicate key to the icebox. Yeah, that's right. It must have been the strawberries.

Ilsa: What strawberries? Who said anything about strawberries?

Rick: Wrong movie. Sorry.

Ilsa reaches across the small table and holds Rick's hands. They lock onto each other's eyes. Rick's stomach gurgles loudly. He looks down and smiles, embarrassed.

Rick: Just listen to that stomach of mine.

Ilsa: Why do you insist on talking about your stomach?

Rick: My mistake. Another wrong movie.

Ilsa: When I said I would never leave you.

The gurgling gets much louder. Abruptly, Rick stands up.

Rick: And you never will. Where I'm going, you can't follow. What I've got to do, you can't be any part of. It doesn't take much to see that the problems of three little people don't amount to a hill of *frijoles* in this crazy world. Someday you'll understand that. But now, now . . . *Donde esta el bano, por favor?*

Proposed SMA Summer Olympics Event #6

I Sing the House Electric

Nobody Knows the Spanish I Speak

Concerning how quickly the mighty power source has fallen, resulting in the untimely death of our circuit breakers, and the challenges of dealing with utility companies

I woke up this morning with nothing to do, and by the end of the day I got only half of it done.

It was a common expat complaint in San Miguel. If you completed one goal during the course of a day, you were considered accomplished. If you finished two things, you were an over-achiever. But if you defied the laws of expat life and somehow completed three or more things during a single day, by God, you were a rock star! And it's not because there was a shortage of Type-A people wandering the cobblestones. On the contrary, the expat community was, pardon the expression, filthy with former CEOs, vice presidents, professors, and entrepreneurs. It was just that no matter what you might have planned for a day, something or someone always popped up, taking your day in a different direction than originally planned.

For many expats it was often hard to remember which day of the week it was, let alone the actual date. I proudly counted myself in that distracted group. And although the expat community heavily skewed toward seniors, the forgetting had less to do with memory loss and more to do with an unscheduled, uncontrollable life. In short, our San Miguel days could assume their own weight, shape, form, and momentum, regardless of our intentions. Put another way, in Mexico we neither took time for granted nor tapped our feet impatiently whenever we found ourselves at the end of a long line. Time may not have been of the essence in Mexico but it was, well, still time—and what was known as "Mexican Time" at that. As expats, we eventually learned to get over it.

Take, for example, the simple act of paying a bill, in this case an electric bill. The electric company, *Comision Federal de Electricidad*, is a monopoly in Mexico. Monopolies, you might recall from your Western Civilization history class, tend to be underachievers in the area of customer service. Because a monopoly is a cross between the only game in town and why buy the cow, there was little reason for such companies to play nice with their customer base. Bills didn't arrive at the same time and power shut-off dates could vary, so it wasn't always easy to know when to pay or how much to fork over. Bills were almost always paid in person, but you could avoid lines by paying your electric bill at a local store, for a small fee. Or, if you have enough extra cash lying around with nothing better for it to do, you could establish an account at a local financial services company, and they would ensure your bills were paid on time. Most people paid their bills upfront and personal.

One time our electric bill appeared not in our mailbox but stuffed in our gate, as if a rival gang had kidnapped the bill, beat it up, rolled it in a cheap rug like a *film noir* corpse and left it in front of our house as a final warning. This happened three days after the bill was officially due. The electric company had a reputation, earned or not, for turning power off if a payment was, say, twenty minutes late. With time and electricity clearly running out, we rushed to our car, drove to the power company office, and queued up with fellow bill-clutchers, pleased to know the office had not yet closed for *comida*, nor had it cut off our service.

That was a good month or two months, since the electric bills came due in two-month cycles.

On another occasion, our electric bill disappeared—or more accurately, never appeared at all. And, as they say about space invaders, we were not alone. It seemed just about every electric bill for neighborhoods in the southern quadrant of San Miguel never made it to its chosen destination.

We eventually learned our electric bills came from Celaya. An electric company employee from that town, new to the company and unfamiliar with the streets of San Miguel, had been assigned to deliver the bills. Quickly frustrated with our streets—a perfectly understandable frustration, by the way—he began stuffing bills in any old gate or throwing them over any old wall. Since it was very windy that day, it was a miracle that any of those bills actually made it to their rightful owners.

At one point, the man decided he had had enough of such nonsense and turned his remaining batch of bills over to an illiterate woman selling *torta* (sandwiches) at a *tienda*. He assured her he would return shortly, and then left town faster than *carnitas* passing through a vegan, leaving the woman with a basket of unreadable bills for people she didn't know. As a result, she did the only logical thing she could do and took the bills home with her. Once the *tienda* owner realized what had happened, he went to her house, retrieved the remaining undelivered bills, and turned them over to the power company. But by this time word had traveled through the expat community and something of a power bill panic set in, sending droves of confused consumers to the power office, where they hoped to get in line before the doors closed for the day, as they routinely did at three P.M.

The telephone company was close to a monopoly in Mexico, and its definition of customer service also could be best described as quixotic. Case in point, shortly after we moved to our second house, the cute little red one, a neighbor told us she had lost phone service. There was a major construction project taking place in La Lejona at the time, and phone service in our little community suddenly dropped, as if individual home service was being picked off and taken out, onesy twosy, by highly trained sharpshooters. She said she lost service after hearing a crackling sound over her phone and that we might want to visit the phone company office if we ever heard the same noise, because the end would be nigh. Not long after her warning, we heard the noise—crackle, crackle, crackle—and promptly visited the phone company. We waited outside an office while one of the employees tapped on his computer and visited with a friend. We were finally let in to see the man, and we explained as best we could our situation.

"Did you call in the problem?" he asked.

"Yes. I left a message a couple of days ago," I said.

"What is your phone number?"

We gave it to him and he typed it into his computer.

"I don't see your message," he said.

"Well, it should be there. I left it," I said.

"It's not here," he said. Then he looked at us suspiciously.

"Look. Could we add it to the computer now, since you're already in the database?" I asked.

"No. You must call from a phone to report a problem," he said.

Arlene took out her cell phone to place the call.

"What's the number," she asked.

"Not a cell phone," he said. "A regular phone. A land-line."

"How can I call from my phone that's not working to report it's not working if it's not working?" I said.

"You use a neighbor's phone," he said.

"But their phone is also out. All the phones are out in our neighborhood," said Arlene.

"I can't help you," he said.

Dramatic pause as we all stared at each other for effect.

"May we speak to the manager?" Arlene asked.

The man introduced us to the manager, a well-dressed, clean-cut, slightly older man in a suit.

"What's the problem?" the manager asked.

We explained the problem.

"Did you report the problem?" he asked.

"That's what we're doing now," I said.

"You must call in the problem," he said.

Arlene and I looked at each other and said, "Hmm."

The manager noticed our displeasure, thought for a moment, then smiled and said, "We have a service phone for emergencies."

We walked over to the phone company's version of the Bat Phone and waited while the manager dialed a number. No answer. He dialed again. No answer. Again, no answer. The manager kept calling the number, with the same result: he could not get through to his own emergency service call center from inside his own office using the official company service phone designed specifically to perform that very act. The now embarrassed manager assured us he would take care of it. And days later he did.

Our roof stored both a gas tank and a water tank but offered no easy access to either from the street. Every two to three months we called the gas company, and they'd bring a truck to our house and fill the tank, which meant a lot of nasty looks from the gas guys—the same guys and the same looks every time—while they dragged out a ladder, then climbed our roof. Their extra effort always resulted in a larger than average tip, so all's well that ends well.

The water was stored in what's called a *tinaco*, which is a big plastic container that looks like a typist's upside-down bottle of Wite-Out, only in black, much larger, and without the brush. The water was on the roof, the water heater on the ground. The water had to first pass down, via gravity, to warm up and then travel back up to our second floor to fill the tub. And it was a beautiful tub, too, perfect for soaking in while reading a book. Unfortunately, the water did not travel well or fast and you could finish a short book before the tub had enough water in it to cover a short body. By that time, of course, the hot water had already turned cold, and you were looking for a different book to read.

I should mention of all the utility companies in San Miguel, the water company was the most efficient and reliable. Paying your water bill was a ten-minute investment of your time. However, we received the best service from the cable company, a concept that was totally out of any *norteamericano's* experience, especially my own.

One morning, we woke up and noticed someone had painted in black the letter "S" inside of a circle on our outer wall, next to the gate. If it were a gang tagging the neighborhood, it was the Gang that Couldn't Paint Straight because the work was very unimaginative; the good news was, almost every house on our street had the same graffiti painted on it.

At first we all thought the guilty party was one of the two water bottle delivery companies, since the company's name began with the letter S. Even the local police thought so. That is, until a neighbor uncovered the real culprit: the tax collecting agency for the local government. Annual property taxes were due at the end of that particular month, and those who had not already paid (in other words, had not paid their taxes early) had their houses painted with the big S in a reverse sort of Passover. Don't skip this house. Apparently, nobody in local government thought that painting on someone's wall without permission was, say, defacing private property. But I guess it's easier than mailing, dropping off an actual tax bill, or knocking on a door. And it did get everyone's attention.

In many ways, living in Mexico was like living in Bizarro World, where the only contractor who reliably showed up on time was the cable guy and the nicest drivers in town were the guys driving the cabs. It was where three prong outlets were the same as two prong outlets and the phone company expected you to use a neighbor's phone—not your own mobile phone—to call in an outage, even though the entire neighborhood was without telephone service.

Whenever I found myself frustrated by the way things worked or didn't work, I was reminded of the final words spoken to the devastated Jack Nicholson character in the movie *Chinatown*:

"Forget it, Jake. It's Chinatown."

But we were in Mexico. And my name wasn't Jake.

Another Art Opening in San Miguel

Frida's Just Another Word for Nothing Left to Paint

 *In which I discuss the incredible art scene in San Miguel, Arlene enrolls in an art class, and I create a weekly cartoon panel about expats*

San Miguel de Allende is a town of, by, and for artists, and Frida Kahlo is its unofficial patron saint, second only to Our Lady of Guadalupe in fame and fortune. With all due respect to Frida, the influential Hispanic artist, her image is as common as Mickey Mouse in Disneyland. Pictures of Frida adorn handbags, blouses, scarves, mirrors, books, posters, postcards, kitchen tiles, kitschy art, and fine art, among other things.

And why not? A major online media site listed the top ten places for art in the entire world, and San Miguel came in at number eight, just after Rome and ahead of Vienna. That impressive standing between two of Europe's finest cultural havens was based on the artists, as well as the art, available in this community of give or take 100,000 residents. Unlike Rome and Vienna, the ranking was not based on the presence of fine art museums, since San Miguel doesn't have any, world famous or otherwise.

What it does have, however, is nearly a year-long supply of sunshine, ideal for traditional outdoor painters, as well as an amazing capacity for absorbing artists and craftspeople from around the world. Two art schools, in particular, continue to draw students who like to draw: *Instituto Allende* and *Bellas Artes*.

Positioned on level ground south and west of the historic Centro, the *Instituto Allende* is one of San Miguel's educational success stories. It serves as both a school of art and a language school, with an increasing number of its students enrolling in the latter. An American, Sterling Dickinson, was instrumental in creating the school and helped bring in many art students from the United States shortly after World War II, helping to boost both the economy and reputation of San Miguel. There's a statue of Mr. Dickinson on one of the busier streets, and a street named in his honor.

Closer to the center of town is the *Instituto Nacional de Bellas Artes*, commonly referred to as *Bellas Artes*, one of the better fine art schools in Mexico, and housed in a former nunnery that dates back to 1775. The two-story building surrounds a huge and gorgeous courtyard, and includes several classrooms, meeting rooms, and art galleries, as well as a small restaurant. It's also the perfect place to sip coffee and treat your eyes and ears to the natural delights of San Miguel.

Arlene and I both love art, and it's one of the reasons we moved to San Miguel. But her last hands-on artistic experience took place in elementary school, where she made animal-like things out of *papier-mâché*, getting all wet and gooey in the process. Once we were in Mexico, where reinventing your self is *de rigueur*, it was time for Arlene to open the doors to her creative spirit and see what was inside.

What was inside, as it turned out, was ceramic. Arlene made ceramic pears, some as beautiful as a Cézanne painting, and others as misshapen as any real pear discarded on the ground. In addition to her ceramic pears, Arlene made several other interesting pieces, including a very realistic-looking sitting, pear-shaped hog and an avant-garde sculpture of a nude woman sitting like a pear. We now refer to that time in her life as her Pear Period.

I was proud of Arlene for signing up for a ceramics class at *Bellas Artes*. She was the only non-Mexican and non-artist in the class, and she toughed it out, even registering for a second term. It proved to be quite the sacrifice, especially since the nine A.M. class really didn't get started until ten A.M. and required at least three coffee breaks, the first beginning at nine-thirty, for socializing is an important part of the culture down here and you dare not skip out. Put another way, the sullen, loner artist with a chip on his shoulder and an axe with which to grind it need not apply to art school in San Miguel. There's no room for sour pusses, especially when the sun is shining so much of the time.

Inspired by Arlene's commitment to reinvent herself, I decided to return to my cartoonish roots and reclaim my inner adolescent. I began drawing a weekly cartoon panel about the expat experience for *Atención*, San Miguel's largest bi-lingual weekly newspaper and have included samples in this book. I titled the panel *Más o Menos*, translated as "More or Less," to reflect the mixed feelings I had about living as an expat. Don't get me wrong, I loved living in Mexico but, at times, still wondered what I was doing in the middle of a foreign country.

In drawing the panel, I limited myself to two rules. The first was that I would never make fun of the Mexican people because they had been so gracious and generous to us.

For my other rule, I would never draw anything political that would give these nice Mexican people a reason for putting me in a not-so nice Mexican jail. At that point in my life, I couldn't afford any jail time. I was too old to be some cellmate's bitch and would have to be his mother.

For a short while, I became something of a very minor celebrity of the seventh order. People would stop me in town and give me an idea for my next cartoon. As you can guess, many of the ideas were unusable. They'd suggest a Cecil B. DeMille scene with a cast of thousands. Or, worse, an idea that was sure to result in the loss of my visa and land me some jail time.

San Miguel was all about art that was happening at the moment. In a typical copy of *Atención*, you could find ads for art classes or gallery openings, sprinkled between the local plastic surgery ads (might have been worth a shot) and brain surgery ads (I passed, though you wouldn't know it), all vastly outnumbered by the seductive and ever-present real estate ads. I could have learned to take better photographs, created my own mosaic, explored printmaking, experimented with collage, mastered batiks or encaustics, made jewelry using only beads and wire, or built a window to the soul, also known as a Mexican *tin nicho* or box. Or I could have kept it simple, with classes in such old standbys as oil, acrylic, or watercolor painting, or three times a week taken an hour-long life-drawing class using my own charcoal sticks, drawing pad, and bifocals. If I considered myself beyond the artist's training-wheel stage, I could have rented space to paint, with good, natural light and an easel maybe included in my rent. The options for creating art or improving your craft seemed endless.

But the big events and the ones we tried to attend were the gallery openings, with your choice of a glass of white or red wine, sometimes even champagne or prosecco, and a chance to meet the artist.

A former turn-of-the-20th-century fabric factory, *La Fabrica La Aurora*, was the town's showcase for high-end art and design. Once a month, Aurora, as it's commonly referred to, held an Art Walk, where new work was presented, accompanied by select snacks and drinks. According to the Aurora web site, the family that owns the building switched from "cotton to the imagination" as their raw material of choice in 2001. Thursdays were open studio days, in which you could meet the various artists in their respective studios or galleries.

A different outlet, known as The Artisan's Market was open seven days a week, and ran the length of a couple of streets. It featured stalls selling hand-made crafts and souvenirs. You could find everything from fake wax fruit to real diamond necklaces. There was plenty of something for everyone and the prices seemed reasonable.

On one particular Saturday night, across town from both Aurora and The Artisan's Market, an artist friend was to have her first art gallery opening. We were all excited for her. Our friend's art was intriguing, striking, and full of passion, very much in the realm of People's Art, consisting mostly of dramatic paintings of indigenous women from around the world. Ah, would that her appetizers were half as good. In a noble gesture typical of our friend's generous heart, rather than use a local professional caterer, she hired a neighborhood woman who had never catered before but wanted to give it a try, thinking it could open up a world of new business opportunities. Unfortunately, the novice caterer's definition of what constituted a proper catered event was based on 1950's middle-America. Her appetizers consisted of Velveeta cheese on soggy crackers, a few cut vegetables (were they washed in filtered water, we all wondered, staying away just in case?), old salsa (I imagine the only way to tell salsa is old is when the red turns green), and the most disappointing collection of tortilla chips this side of Salt Lake City.

All would be forgiven if the drinks lived up to expectations, but the punch lacked punch, since the caterer wannabe even scrimped on the tequila, as close as one gets to committing a mortal sin in Mexico. On the shoals of such appetizers, many a promising art career had floundered and fallen to the murky depths, never to recover. Purple prose aside, our friend and her art survived the night, and she went on to show her work in other galleries in both Mexico and the United States.

That one night of lousy appetizers was an exception, however, for in most cases art openings in San Miguel provided some of the best—and certainly cheapest—food and drink in town, and often included live entertainment, some guy on a piano, some woman with a cello. An expat could easily plan his or her evening meals around such gallery openings, especially during the peak winter months when openings were as common as firecrackers, and grazing for free food was corollary to art appreciation.

But art in San Miguel was not limited to galleries and stalls. The houses themselves were painted canvases, with their multi-colored facades, each hiding a home and garden worthy of a magazine feature article or its own book. Bright color combinations were the norm: a whimsical yellow house with orange highlights, lime green sliced by a blue bar, a duo of half rusty red and half bright white. These were the kind of residential facades outlawed by every Covenant Condition Restriction (CC&R) document in America.

Inside, homes often showcased an eclectic collection of indigenous and contemporary art. Landscape art was also well represented in San Miguel, and with a year-around growing season, there was never a shortage of foliage to admire or covet. In short, the town reeked of art, and one couldn't help but get caught up and taken in by the visual beauty of it all.

San Miguel has been called the "Florence of Mexico," implying its similarity to the Italian town known as the center of the Renaissance. Or on second thought maybe they were referring to one of my aunts, long since dead, who would have felt right at home in this town of artist first-timers and bona-fides, nodding with an experienced eye at the latest gallery paintings, munching on appetizers, clutching a cup of punch close to her chest.

And now back to Frida. She was an inspirational artist and person, especially since she had to deal with Diego Rivera's massive ego, not to mention his massive body. She was bisexual. It's said she had affairs with communism's most eligible married man in exile, Leon Trotsky, as well as the famous jazz singer Josephine Baker, among others. She was enormously talented and brave, and lived the full, chaotic, mercurial life of an artist, even though she was overshadowed, at times, by a man. She developed polio at an early age and, a few years later, was severely injured in a traffic accident. She suffered great physical pain throughout her life, dying far too soon at the age of 47, and about a third of her paintings were self-portraits, wildly colorful and deliberately symbolic. With a life like that, is it any wonder the spirit of Frida continues to inspire?

Frida Kahlo said of her own work, "I never paint dreams or nightmares. I paint my own reality." For many art lovers in San Miguel, reality comes with appetizers.

**Winners of the Expat
Frida Kahlo Look-a-Like Contest**

Temptation, Thy Name is DVD

In which I'm introduced to the evil allure of the black market, succumb, shamefully abuse copyright law, and am appropriately and justly punished for my sins

"Boy, do I feel like an idiot. I rented a bunch of movies, and they didn't work in my DVD player," I told my expat neighbor and Mexico-lifestyle mentor, George.

"Didn't anyone tell you to not rent Region 4 films?" George asked. "Those only work in DVD players bought in Mexico."

"I know now."

'Why rent anyway, it's cheaper to buy."

"You can buy movies here?"

"You bet. Not just any movies, first-run theatrical releases. I bought *The DaVinci Code* two weeks after it was released to theaters."

If I could whistle on demand, I would have whistled. Instead, the only time I whistle I really don't mean to do it. More often than not, a whistle-like sound comes out of my mouth when I least expect it, thanks to a combination of the natural aging process and early years of cheap dental care. This time? No whistle.

"Ah, black market videos." I nodded.

"No, Tuesday Market. And they're DVDs, not videos."

Why didn't I think of that before? You could buy anything at Tuesday Market (*Tianguis del Martes*), from live chickens to dead auto parts. It was like that song "Alice's Restaurant," where you can get anything you want *excepting Alice*. And the market was actually open only on Tuesdays, unlike the Saturday Market we left behind in Portland, which was also open on Sundays and for extended days from Thanksgiving through Christmas Eve, hoping to squeeze the last sale out of the last consumer.

"There are plenty of stalls to buy from. I like the Movie Guy by the Fish Guy. You know him?" George asked.

"Of course," I said, meaning I knew the Fish Guy.

Tuesday Market, a cross between a farmers' market and flea market with some arts and crafts thrown in, covered a wide expanse, mostly under gigantic tents, with extra vendors on its outskirts, hawking everything from designer jeans to designer watches, from candy bars to chile peppers to whole chickens, even whole live ones, and all consumer points in-between. As big and hectic as Tuesday Market was, everyone knew the Fish Guy. He was better known than even the *Mole* Guy, a man who sold the popular chile pepper-based paste out of buckets. We were more than five hours from the ocean, thousands of feet up, in the middle of a semi-arid region surrounded by mountains, but there was one soul willing to truck in fish from Veracruz and sell it at Tuesday Market: Ladies and Gentlemen, I give you the *pescadero* stylings of the Fish Guy.

So even I knew where the Fish Guy sold his wares, and I'd only been to Tuesday Market twice, both times as the family *burro*. In our family, I not only opened jars, I carried things. As spouse, it was my sworn duty, one I gladly accepted and took seriously.

But *this* (cue the John Williams score) was about ... the Movies.

The parking lot was football-field-large, dotted with protruding rocks and sunken holes and clogged with shoppers. If you got there too late but early enough to park in a regular spot, you could emerge from the market an hour later only to find someone parked directly behind you, blocking your exit. Late arrivals parked in a long line that separated the normal rows of parked cars while running perpendicular to them. If you narrowed your eyes and thought of a bad haircut, then looked at the line of randomly parked cars, what came to mind was that long hangy-down part of a mullet.

"Where are you going?" Arlene said as we entered the first tent.

"It's a secret," I said. "I'll meet you at the chicken place in a few minutes."

Arlene wandered off to do her usual shopping, picking up veggies, fruits, tamales, and, of course, chicken. I, on the other hand, went looking for the Movie Guy, who was hiding out somewhere between the Fish Guy and the *Mole* Guy, and it wasn't long before I found him.

The movie titles were challenging, since they were all in Spanish and not always what you would consider to be a one-for-one translation. For example, the popular American musical *Grease* in Spanish became *Vaselina*. I picked a romance flick for the both of us, mostly for Arlene. I also grabbed a broad comedy for both of us but mostly for me, an action thriller for me, and an inane teenage comedy for the dog. They were all new movies, still in theatrical release, and all for less than the equivalent of ten U.S. dollars. What a deal, I told myself, having forgotten you get what you pay for in life, even at Tuesday Market.

That night, I told Arlene I had a special surprise. We were going to watch movies, and not just any movies but first-run, theatrical-release flicks. In honor of the occasion, I made popcorn in the microwave, poured two glasses of wine, and pulled the drapes shut.

I decided to start with my strongest suit and inserted the romance film as featured movie number one. Unfortunately, the sound was out of sync with the visual. It reminded us both of the scene from *Singing in the Rain* when a Hollywood studio tried to make the transition from silent films to talkies and failed miserably.

"I can't watch this," Arlene said.

I couldn't either, I thought.

"No problem. We have three other movies to choose from," I said, as I cheerfully removed DVD #1 from the disc player and inserted DVD #2.

DVD #2 introduced a new, albeit not so minor, problem. The only languages available on the disc were Spanish, French, and Portuguese, and since both Arlene and I still struggle with English, it was a no-go from the get-go. I pulled movie #2 out of the player and set it aside. "Sorry," I said sheepishly.

I removed DVD #3 from its sleeve and looked it over carefully, as if I knew what I was doing. But it appeared to be like all the others: a generic white DVD without a label in a box as thin as a pancake.

"This one looks okay," I said, and inserted our third movie of the night into the machine.

It was obvious that DVD #3 was being copied from inside a theater. The shadow of a big guy sitting in front and slightly to the right of the camera tipped us off. But we continued to watch the movie, hoping for some improvement, and all went well until we reached a sequence that was particularly confusing. The hero, who was more of an anti-hero but nonetheless comic book heroic, started coughing and sneezing. He made deep, bronchitis-like spasms. The noise was unexpected and I couldn't believe my ears or eyes. One minute this guy was dispatching evil totalitarian government agents, left and right, willy-nilly, as if flicking lint from a suit. The next minute he was dying of tuberculosis, like a scene out of *Le Boheme*. Who knew he was that sick? Then I understood what was going on. The hero in the film was not hacking like a two-pack-a-day smoker. It was the guy copying the movie inside of the movie house. The illegal copyist needed the gig and couldn't afford to call in sick. I stopped movie #3 and took it out of the DVD player. Three down, one to go.

"Four's the charm," I told Arlene.

"How much did you pay for these?" asked Arlene, using her skeptical voice.

I assumed her question to be rhetorical and continued to insert DVD #4 into the disc player. We were down to our last film, the inane teenage comedy. Oddly enough, this one was in English and the sound on it was near-perfect, which was half of the battle. But—and there's always a but with these things—the movie looked as if it had been filmed under water and through a curtain. After several minutes of intense viewing, the kind of concentration that can result in a brain tumor, I looked at Arlene and she nodded. I removed the disc from the player.

"I think I'll go up to bed and read," said Arlene.

"Popcorn?" I offered.

She shook her head no and wandered up the stairs, leaving me alone to contemplate four dead DVDs and an entire bowl of the stuff.

If my years in Catholic school taught me anything, they taught me how to fret and stew and feel guilty late into the night. I couldn't sleep. I thought about how, so many years before, when I was in the United States Navy assigned to the Seabees, I spent my last night on Diego Garcia, a tiny atoll in the middle of the Indian Ocean, at an ad hoc adult film festival where sleazy movies were being shown in honor of three men who were returning home to the States in the morning—for good. We were short-timers, and were soon to swap our military lives for civilian ones.

Our friend, a postal clerk petty officer, put together the festival and charged admission. As his guests of honor, we did not have to pay, of course, but everyone else did. The room was packed. Our petty officer friend was the entrepreneurial type. He showed films as one of his many business-making side ventures while in the Navy. He was a big man, in both body and vision, and carried the nickname of Four-by-Four, a name earned the time he went back during the same breakfast four times for four eggs each time, the maximum number allowed per person per pass through the chow line.

All did not go as Four-by-Four had planned that night. The first film ended abruptly just after a man and a woman began to fondle and kiss each other. The second film also ended prematurely, no pun intended, with barely a naked breast to be seen. The third and fourth films followed the same pattern, as did the fifth, and by this time the natives were restless. Seabees started asking for their money back and filing out, grousing under their breath as they made their way to the enlisted men's bar. Apparently, our entrepreneurial friend had received a batch of teaser films, sent to entice him to buy the real films, and he had not taken the time to preview what he had received.

In the morning, I grabbed the black market DVDs and threw them in the garbage can. Then I logged onto the Internet and subscribed to Netflix, for five movies at a time, knowing I'd much rather have the real thing than be teased by mere glimpses of what could be. In my salad days, I would have rushed to confession. But the confessional door was no longer open to me, so I did the next best thing. I washed my hands. Within hours, I no longer felt dirty. I was back to being another law-abiding, neurotic fan of movies, waiting impatiently for his first red Netflix envelope to arrive.

Proposed SMA Summer Olympics Event #2

I Like St. Mike

 *In which we get up at two in the morning to join a wild birthday party downtown and why, even at our age, it was all worth it in the end*

Growing up Catholic I had plenty of heroes to emulate, but my heroes rarely won any battles. In fact, they almost always lost, opting instead for martyrdom, which made for interesting, if not confusing, role models.

I can't imagine Vince Lombardi, for example, telling his famous Green Bay Packers to take off their helmets and shoulder pads, and stand perfectly still and smile while the opposing team charged full force across the line of scrimmage.

But at least we always had St. Michael the Archangel, and he was an action figure in the best sense of the word. You never saw paintings of a quivering, frightened St. Michael raising his arms and mouthing the words, "I surrender," or dropping his weapon and hightailing it away from a fight. On the contrary, he was usually painted or carved in mid-battle, swinging a sword as he clobbered one of Lucifer's captains or, in most cases, the villainous scum Lucifer himself. The archangel was never on the bench, *hors de combat*. He was a player.

And so the residents of San Miguel de Allende, St. Michael's namesake city, have every reason to be proud of their patron saint and rightly do not hold back when it comes time to celebrate his birthday. The event is called *La Alborada*, Spanish for "dawn," and it's the kind of prolonged celebration that makes homecoming week at the University of Alabama seem like a giant nap by comparison. A uniquely San Miguel fiesta, it unites pagan and Catholic symbols and rites into an amazing wee-hours-of-the-morning display of fireworks, tradition, dance, faith, and tamales.

And did I mention the partying isn't over in a single night? Celebrating can go on for a week, several days before *La Alborada* and a day or two after or as long as it takes to pay due homage to San Miguel's municipal patron. In fact, it seems the exact duration of a fiesta in Mexico is much like the exact measurement of anything in this country: elusive.

The climactic event, however, is the knock-out, drag-down, winner-take-all fight between St. Michael and Lucifer. The battle takes place on Saturday from four A.M. to five A.M. in *El Jardin* and in front of the town's famous Gaudi-like church *La Parroquia*. Saint Michael wins, of course, and at the end of the battle, everyone sings "Happy Birthday" to the archangel. He makes a wish, blows out the candles, and everyone goes home, confident that once again Good has triumphed over Evil. But I'm getting ahead of myself.

On the night before *La Alborada*, we set our alarm for two A.M., wanting to arrive early enough at *El Jardin* to get a good taste of the festivities before the rockets red glare began. But when the alarm went off, there were no fireworks in our little corner of the world. In fact, it was deathly still, with the exception of a few pitiful human moans.

We remained snug in our bed more asleep than awake, as we struggled to debate the merits of crawling out and getting dressed, driving into town, parking, walking up the hill, and joining what we knew ahead of time would be a huge and boisterous crowd of party-goers. A mob. For there was this other thought under serious consideration: We could simply turn off the light and go back to sleep. Hmm. It was a debate for the ages—or for the aged—and it went along these lines:

Me: "Damn. It can't be two already?"

I turned on my nightstand light, squinted, rubbed my eyes, squinted some more, and fell back in bed. Arlene instinctively pulled the covers high over her body.

Arlene: "Whaffmppghfhgpffff?"

Me: "Wha?"

Arlene: "What time is it?"

Me: "Time to get up."

Arlene: "Are you sure?"

Me: "Sure about what?"

Arlene: "Sure you want to do this?"

Me: [slight pause] "No."

I turned the light back off and crawled under the blanket. After a few seconds, Arlene turned her nightstand light on. She paused before speaking, as if thinking it through and choosing her words carefully.

Arlene: "Get up."

Me: "What?"

Arlene: "We have to go. We told Karen we'd meet her."

Me: "She's probably not going to be there, anyway."

Arlene: "It's once a year and we've never been to it before."

Me: "Every day is once a year."

Arlene: "You're not making any sense."

Me: "I'm not supposed to make sense. I'm sleeping."

Arlene: "We should go. It's St. Michael's birthday, after all."

Me: "You're not Catholic."

Arlene: "That's not the point."

Me: "The point is, it's two in the morning and we're both pushing sixty."

Arlene: "The point, is we didn't move down here just to sleep. We moved here to experience things. Life. Culture— "

Me: —Sleep. We're in the land of *siestas*."

Arlene: "Then we can take a nap later in the day. This is going to be fun."

I knew I had lost the battle as soon as the alarm sounded, but I was stalling. When you're sleepy, especially when an alarm shocks you awake in the middle of the night, every fraction of a second of shut-eye counts a hundredfold. In such situations, an extra five minutes can mean as much as two hours of regular sleep. I'm not a sleep scholar, and I certainly don't understand the math of it all, but trust me: I needed five more minutes of sleep. But it wasn't going to happen.

Soon we found ourselves walking up a narrow, dark street leading to the town square, part of a crush of celebrants inching along. Was I the only one wondering what the hell I was doing up so late or so early? And how do you know when you're staying up too late or getting up too early anyway? Is there a pre-determined time, a line of demarcation between too late and too early? Why does a weather forecaster call one day "partly sunny' and the next day, with seemingly the same exact weather conditions, "partly cloudy"? Even when I'm wide-awake such minor mysteries of life confuse me. Half asleep, I was hopeless.

We arrived at the town's main plaza and squeezed ourselves in with the masses, at first huddling under the portal surrounding the square. Then we scooted into the middle of the plaza for a better view of the action. This was not the smartest place to stand, as it turned out, for we were soon crushed together like grapes; canned jalapenos, to mix my food metaphors, had more room. Teenagers mingled with their friends, parents with their kids, twenty-somethings with forty-somethings, forty-somethings with sixty-somethings, and sixty-somethings with whatever was left. Mothers held babies, husbands hugged wives. And I'm sure more than one pocket was picked.

Then the battle started.

At one end of the square, rockets were launched high into the air. Directly below this light show, the sight was spectacular, noise deafening, and smell overpowering. It was difficult to imagine Hell itself having more sulfur than San Miguel at that moment.

In front of *La Parroquia*, wooden towers (*castillos*) made by Indian craftsmen were covered with fireworks and rocket-propelled pinwheels. When the fuses were lit, rockets blasted up and onto the street, bouncing off nearby buildings as fireworks shot into the sky. It was both awe-inspiring and hilarious at the same time, something a mid-century American boy might expect from a collaboration between Wile E. Coyote and The Acme Corporation.

So there we were, in the thick of it. Rockets red-glared. Music loud-blared. Smoke billowed-thick. Nobody was going gentle into that good night. Before long the streets were littered with the debris of spent fireworks, and all present were covered with the sulfurous residue. We could neither see nor hear each other, and my mind began to wonder once again: Where do they get their fireworks? In all our driving through Mexico we never once saw a fireworks stand or fireworks warehouse. This was going to remain one of life's mysteries.

Then just as suddenly, the battle ended.

With dead rockets littering the ground and noxious smoke swirling like a scene out of the *Hound of the Baskervilles*, it was time to sing "Happy Birthday" to the victorious Saint, followed by a round of robust cheering. Then it was off to home. The crowd, still festive, began to straggle down the narrow side streets. We joined in, and along the way we stopped, as did many others, and bought tamales from a small vendor, as well as *atole*, a pre-Hispanic corn-based drink. Fighting Evil, it seems, was good for the appetite. By the time we made it to our house on the outskirts of town, the sun was already up, the sky already showing signs of another glorious clear day ahead. And we were, without a doubt, thoroughly exhausted.

But this was life in San Miguel, and we knew we were just getting started. We set our alarm for nine A.M. We didn't want to miss the rest of the celebrations scheduled for Saturday, a day full of parades and dances by the various, colorfully dressed Indian tribes. Dozens of floats carrying large floral arrangements of cactus and flowers (called *xúchiles*) would make their way to *La Parroquia*, where they would be mounted for all to see.

And, of course, we didn't want to miss the pre-Hispanic ceremony of the *Voladores de Papantla* (the flyers of Papantla). These "birdmen" would climb to the top of a very tall pole and spiral downward—a rope attached to their feet—until they reached the ground, a pre-Yuppie form of bungee jumping with neither net nor river below.

Sunday was not to be missed, either: another day of parades, with large puppets, called *Mojigangas*, leading the way, followed by numerous Indian tribes in traditional dress. The plaza was jammed on both days as onlookers, in some places five deep, watched the various parades pass by. It was a huge feast for the senses. The drumming, rattling, and shaking of various traditional instruments blended with bright colors and large feathered head-dresses, and, in some cases, burning incense.

Officially, the Feast of St. Michael the Archangel is on September 29, but in reality the feast involves at least one week of non-stop cultural activities. We stopped after three days.

We had no regrets about getting up at two A.M. for a crazy birthday party in honor of an angel and thrown by a thousand of his closest friends and would do it again—in a heartbeat, as long as our hearts were still beating. Besides, if good ol' St. Mike could tolerate the flash and smoke and stench and noise and falling debris and crying babies and drunk daddies and confused expats, well then, so could we. It was the least we could do for the Man (make that Angel) who Shot (make that Speared) Lucifer Valance.

We looked everywhere in the *Jardin* for Karen in the early morning hours on Saturday but couldn't find her and only later learned she had elected to sleep in.

Alternative Use #3 for Nopals

Sometimes Life Really is a Cabaret

 Concerning our efforts to get out more at night and do things in town, resulting in a close encounter with disco in a Mexican nightclub and why Bette Davis keeps looking at me

"I sure miss getting a daily newspaper," Arlene said, as she turned the pages of a laser-printed eight and a half by eleven inch copy of an article from an online version of the day's *New York Times*.

"It's the same news we'd be getting in Portland," I answered, rather unconvincingly. I squinted up at Arlene from my own stack of laser-printed articles.

"Not the same at all. The same information, yes, but not the same experience," she said.

And I knew she was right. Arlene was almost always right, an occasional source of friction in our marriage since I hate being almost always wrong. But in this rare case, we were eventually both right and agreed that it would, indeed, be nice in the morning to drink coffee and turn the pages of a real newspaper, struggling with the folds and creases, just as we had for so many years in the United States. We set down our respective pages, sipped our coffee, and didn't talk for several minutes, letting our minds wander off to wherever minds wander off to early in the morning.

"What do you miss most about Portland?" I asked, finally breaking the silence.

"Not counting friends?" Arlene asked.

"Or relatives," I said.

"I miss the wonderful food stores," Arlene said, without hesitation, a true gourmet stepping up to the dinner plate.

"The cheeses," I added.

"The meats," she threw in.

By then we were off and running.

"The seafood."

"Especially Dungeness crab."

"God, I love Dungeness crab."

"The best."

"The wines."

"Bookstores."

"Especially Powell's."

"Movie houses."

"Tall, green trees."

"Farmers' markets."

"The Trailblazers."

"The half-yearly sale at Nordies."

"The rain. Ha. Just kidding," I added quickly.

"Portland has such a great ethnic restaurant scene. It's a town made for foodies," Arlene said.

"One of the best," I took another long sip from my coffee mug.

"I miss not having to soak all my fruits and vegetables in iodine. Or using tap water when brushing my teeth," Arlene added.

I had a feeling we could add to the list for a long time and we would both be better served if the list were kept short.

"What is the one thing you miss most?" I reiterated, returning to the intent of my original question.

"If I have to limit it to one thing," Arlene said, stopping between clauses for dramatic effect, "what I miss most is ballet."

She nailed it again. With the exception of men and women randomly falling in the uneven streets of San Miguel, there was little in town that might appeal to hoofer lovers and Arlene loved dance, especially ballet. However, dance wasn't even on the same continent as my wish list, let alone on the top of it.

"What do you miss most about the States?" Arlene asked.

"I really miss live theater," I said, deciding to stick with the performing arts category.

"Oh, really? What exactly do you miss?"

I flashed back to five years earlier. I had started writing and sending out short plays in my spare time, with modest success. It was late June, and we were in New York City for the premiere of two of my plays as part of a festival of short works performed in an off-off Broadway venue in the heart of the Theater District. The black box theater was on the same street as many popular Broadway theaters, just a couple of blocks away from the big boys. We arrived the night before my play and walked past the St. James Theatre, where *The Producers*, then starring Nathan Lane and Matthew Broderick, was running. I noticed a crowd waiting between the stage door exit and a parked limo and asked Arlene if we could stop for a few minutes. Just then, Mr. Lane ran out of the theater and into the limo. I looked across the street and waved at him. Our eyes met, and I said, "Yo, Lane," and he said, "Yo, Saunders."

Or at least that's how I like to think it happened, but in fact it was raining, and he had merely raised an arm to shield himself as he scooted into the back seat of his ride. Our eyes never met; we never spoke. Nonetheless, I was thrilled to see Mr. Lane, who was playing Max Bialystock, on the night before I was to see a production of my first play, make that two plays, as a new part-time playwright in the center of America's theater scene. In a perverse sort of way I saw it as a positive omen: Max Bialystock, he whose plays were said to close on the first day of rehearsal.

A few days later, we had tickets for a Sunday matinee to see a real Broadway production, unlike my off-off stuff. We were staying in a small hotel that reeked of boutique charm: compact rooms, disinterested staff, a shower with arbitrary hot water, quite possibly the slowest elevator in mid-town Manhattan. Dressed in our go-to-theater finery and sitting in our cramped room waiting to leave, Arlene handed me the envelope with our tickets and asked me to recheck the play's location and time. I opened the newspaper and confirmed we were a mere three blocks away, with a three P.M. curtain time.

At ten minutes after two we stood, walked to the elevator, took the slow ride from the fifth floor to the first, then pushed our way through a line of theater-goers on our street and headed for a different line of theater-goers a few streets over. It was hot, muggy, crowded. It was New York City in summer and The Big Apple was being baked.

We arrived at the venue and blended with the crowd, waiting for the doors to open.

"Where are our seats?" Arlene asked, innocently enough.

I reached into my pocket to pull out the tickets. Nothing. I reached in another pocket. Nothing. I checked my remaining pockets, long-shots all, and my ruddy complexion must have turned fish-belly white. "I don't have the tickets," I said.

"You must have them. I gave them to you in the room."

We stared at each other, not speaking. Then I did what any red-blooded American husband would have done. I looked Arlene straight in the eye and said, "Whatever possessed you to give me the tickets in the first place?"

Arlene was about to counter with what any red-blooded American wife would say, casting a lethal finger in my direction. But I stopped her. I reached over and put my hand over her poised finger gently and said, "You're right. It's my fault. I must have left the envelope in the room. If I hurry, I can get the tickets and be back in time."

"Uh," Arlene said, as I turned and dashed off before she could finish her sentence.

I made it to the boutique hotel in record time, rode up the elevator in less than record time, searched the tiny room in record time, and, in record time, found—nothing. The tickets were not there. I would rush back and buy new tickets, if tickets were still available, I told myself, and if that didn't work, I would be prepared to eat crow for the next six months. Being a nincompoop was not easy, but it was a role that suited me.

I left the hotel and started walking back to the theater, head down, dejected, and that's when I spotted a familiar envelope on the ground in front of the hotel. I picked it up, looked inside, and saw our tickets. The envelope must have fallen out of my pocket on our way to the matinee and had gone unnoticed, just another piece of unclaimed debris in the city that never sleeps.

"Thank you, Jesus," I cried, holding the envelope high above me as if I were hoisting a NASCAR trophy. Now I knew I was going to make it, a goat turned hero. I flew, running as fast as I could, pushing my way through mobs of people, bumping into strangers and apologizing while bumping into still more strangers: "Sorry. Sorry. In a hurry. Sorry. Late. Sorry."

Arlene would tell me later that when she saw me run up the street, bulldozing my way through the masses, I looked like both a marvel of determination and a heart attack in process. My thin hair was wet, matted to my thick head. My shirt was untucked and waved behind me as if cheering me on. Beneath my sports coat it was drenched. One set of shoe laces was undone. My clean slacks no longer looked clean or wrinkle-free. And I had started to limp, like Chester Goode from the old *Gunsmoke* television show.

But with a few minutes to spare, I made it to the theater door and to Arlene, who waited alone, for by that time the others were already inside. I bent over, head between my knees to catch my breath, and handed her the tickets. We walked in and stopped at the mezzanine, where I took a few much-needed puffs on my asthma emergency inhaler. It didn't help, for when we took our seats I was still gasping. The lights were up, chatter rampant, the room all a-buzz. Suddenly the lights dimmed, everyone stopped talking, and the room turned very quiet. The play was about to begin, but awful, painful, loud sounds came out of my chest. I was certain the entire audience could hear me wheeze, especially since the theater offered the kind of acoustical environment one would expect for seventy-five dollar seats. It didn't matter because we were about to watch Gary Sinese star as Randal Patrick McMurphy in *One Flew Over the Cuckoo's Nest*, a play set in an asylum, and the audience probably thought my wheezing was a sound effect.

The play went on, exceeding my expectations. At one point late in the play, the shy asylum patient Billy Bibbit ran off-stage to commit suicide, and an orderly followed him. The orderly called for Nurse Ratchet, who also ran off-stage but returned moments later, her nurse's outfit drenched in blood. A woman behind me in her best-loudest-thickest New Jersey accent screamed: "Oh, my Gawd!" Theater-goers for three rows turned to look at her, as if to say, "Lady, what? You didn't know he was going to kill himself?"

I chuckled to myself at the memory. Arlene repeated her question, pulling me back into the present.

"I said what do you miss about live theater?"

"All of it," I said. "Everything."

"Well, at least you can get some live theater here. I can't get any ballet," she said.

Arlene was right. Again. As always. There were a few theatrical productions in town, from on-going staged readings to performances by expat companies to traveling song-and-dance cabaret shows in bars and coffee shops. Although always very affordable, local productions were often hit and miss, and rarely leading or cutting edge. I do recall seeing a very credible production of *A Man for All Seasons*.

However, I longed for season tickets to an equity company. I missed younger performers, more challenging performances. And I missed the variety, not just the quality. That said, in many ways living in San Miguel was like being on a cruise ship: you could spend all your time sitting in a deck chair reading a thick book or you could be busy from morning to night, moving from one fun-filled activity to the next like a conga line full of double espressos. If I felt bored, it was my own fault.

"There's nothing stopping us from going out on the town," Arlene added. "We've been cocooning in this house for too long."

"It's the beginning of the peak tourist season and there's a lot going on," I said.

"Jan arrives tomorrow. Mary's already here. How about the four of us go out to dinner and then see what's going on in Centro? We can play it by ear."

"Brilliant," I said. Even I was not sure what I meant by the word.

The four of us had a delicious, entertaining dinner at a steak house, after which, on the happy side of inebriation, we bar-hopped through the charming, narrow streets. At one point Mary spotted a disco club and uttered three disturbing words, "Let's go dancing." The only three words in the English language that struck more fear in my heart were the words "Ready to Assemble," and that, of course, is another much longer and sadder story.

We paid our entrance fee, the equivalent of almost six U.S. dollars, were frisked, and then seated at a table on the ground floor, inches away from the dance platform. The night club was circular, with two balconies, and huge fishnets restraining balloons above the floor and ready to drop as soon as Mexico's answer to Dick Clark gave the word. Life-sized posters from the hey-day of disco graced the walls of the upper floors, from Madonna to Travolta, as if the room were a religious shrine and the photos were two-dimensional statues of saints. There was a fog machine and strobe lights, of course. But the joint was not exactly jumping.

A party of Mexicans had pushed smaller tables together adjacent to us and were in the middle of a private fiesta. Two men, thirty-something types, and six younger women, possessing what Arlene called "zero waistlines," were drinking tequila and laughing, laughter being one of tequila's better byproducts. We were served our drinks just as one of the two men began dancing with one of the younger women; soon he was dancing with two, then three of the younger women from his table, all at the same time. He turned and gestured to our table, asking Mary to join them. He didn't have to ask twice, and Mary was soon on the floor, dancing with the group of strangers. Before any of his dancing partners knew it, the man was off at the other end of the room, dancing alone, lost in his own world.

We all watched Mary, now dancing alone and in her own world, and the young girls who were dancing together in their own zero-waistline world, as if surrounding an invisible May pole.

"Come on, let's join Mary. Let's dance," Arlene said.

"You know my rule," I said.

"What rule is that?" Jan asked.

"He won't dance unless a lot of people are already on the floor," Arlene said.

"I'm not a good dancer. In fact, I'm a lousy dancer and don't like people watching me," I explained.

"Nobody's going to care," said Jan.

"Duh," added Arlene.

"Look, it's not going to happen. I'm not going out there and make a fool of myself," I said, even though the fool part of my character had been established long ago. "At least not until more people get out there."

Since most of the customers in the room seemed to be on the dance floor already and the number barely covered a small corner of the floor, I knew I was safe. They would have to bus in dancers from neighboring towns, and by that time we would be home.

But just then a voice boomed over the loudspeaker, rattling off Spanish in quick charges like bullets spitting from a semi-automatic. Fog billowed out of the machine and coasted over the dance floor. Strobe lights rotated above. Suddenly, the floor was packed with dancers, bodies pushing against each other, dancing to American tunes from the leisure-suited era. Where were they hiding, I asked myself, upstairs in the dark balcony? It's as if the emcee had announced free Ford Escorts to the first fifty dancers, and then, bam, the dance floor was packed. However for me, personally and emotionally, it was closer to the gladiators of old saying, "We who are about to die, salute you," for I was busted big time.

I soon found myself sweating with a much younger crowd, gyrating out of tune, moving my legs as if both had nervous ticks, then raising my arms to the lyrics of "Y.M.C.A." and "We Are Family." The four of us were the only non-Mexicans on the dance floor, as far as I could tell, and old enough to be the grandparents of the rest. But Jan and Arlene were right, nobody cared how I danced. I know I didn't. It was groovy, man. (Did I really say that?)

Back home later that night, I couldn't sleep. My legs and arms ached. My chest felt tight. My head spun like a vinyl record. Mostly I couldn't sleep because the voice of Kim Carnes sounding a lot like Rod Stewart ran through my head. Not the entire song, mind you, just the refrain, "She's got Bette Davis eyes." Something about teasing you and uneasing you and pleasing you was in there as well, but the fudge factory inside my head always returned to "She's got Bette Davis eyes." Over and over and over and over. Okay, I get it: she's got her eyes, now please may I close *my* eyes and go to sleep?

The next morning at breakfast I thought of the many things I would miss about San Miguel, should we ever leave and not return. First, there would be the weather, and not just nice, mild, temperate weather, but a sky so intense that if it were a cheese, it would be extra, extra sharp cheddar. The idea of cheese the color of sky didn't appeal to me so early in the morning, so I moved on. I thought of other things I would miss. The brightly-colored houses that made me smile every time I saw them. I'd definitely miss the houses and the people, who are warm and friendly and don't seem to mind whenever I bungle their language. I'd miss the slower pace, daily walks, endless fiestas. I was sure I would miss the occasional Mexican out-of-tune street band marching through town for its enthusiasm alone. I'd miss a doctor who makes house calls and a pharmacy that delivers to your door. The mariachi singers in the town plaza at night would, of course, be impossible to replace. As would our two housekeepers, both affectionate and hardworking and the best housekeepers we've ever had, bar none. And of bars, I'd miss the 2-for-1 drink nights at Harry's, which can quickly become 4-for-1 drink nights if a patron rolls the dice against the bartender and wins while you're lucky enough to be sitting in the same room. The colonial architecture, the sense of history, the brightly lit churches at night, the open-air street markets, the stoic *burros* laden with firewood, the knife-sharpener who walks through the narrow streets whistling for business, the many cultural differences, the delicious *guacamole* and *salsas* and chicken *mole*, the sunsets—I would miss them all.

But I swear on the eyes of Bette Davis, I would not miss disco.

Nobody Knows the Spanish I Speak

Beware of Guests Bearing Gifts

Love Among the Expats

Nobody Knows the Spanish I Speak

A meditation on why some people are better suited to make short visits to Epcot Center than commit to a prolonged stay in a foreign country, and what kind of expat was I, really?

After our first year and a half in San Miguel, I felt another identity crisis coming on. I sat outside in our back courtyard, under a wide tent of blue sky, listening to birds chirp, watching butterflies flit, sipping a beer, and feeling the sun's warmth on my back. But inside I felt empty. What was wrong with me? I mean, other than the obvious bad teeth, no hair, an inability to sleep for more than four hours a night, and an intense fear of scorpions that bordered on the obsessive-compulsive, forcing the two of us to regularly check our bed at night and our shoes in the morning for predatory anthropods on a suicide mission?

I should have been big-musical-number happy with our new life in Mexico. The people were warm and friendly. I was no longer working for the man, as Monty had put it back in Portland. And the weather was darn near perfect. Here there was no point to Little Orphan Annie singing about the sun coming out tomorrow, because it beamed on you every day. Yet something didn't feel right. I couldn't put my finger on it, or anyone else's finger, for that matter. I just wasn't sure what I was doing in the central highlands of Mexico, besides soaking up sun. For reasons beyond my understanding, I still felt unsettled, even after a year, and conducted myself accordingly, more as a tourist than an expat. Deep inside I must have always assumed we wouldn't stay long. In fact, prior to moving to Mexico, I described to several of our Portland friends what we were doing as a "one-year, self-funded sabbatical." I enjoyed San Miguel, the incredible sights, sounds, and smells. Well, maybe not the smells. But I remained aloof and uninvolved in the community. I was still an outsider looking in. The odds of me winning Expat of the Year, long though they were at the beginning of our adventure, had long since dropped off the betting board. Arlene, on the other hand, was doing finer than frog's hair.

So the little squirrels in my brain began running in their cage. Before I knew it, the cage floor was littered with questions. What was I doing in San Miguel? Where did I belong, if not here? Where should I go and what would I do next? Why can't I feel satisfied? If a miracle happened tomorrow and the Oakland Raiders won the Super Bowl, would I still have this empty feeling in my stomach? Or was it just another amoeba? My hourglass was running out of sand. Bliss seemed amiss. Faintly, I began to hear "What's it all about, Alfie" playing again in the jukebox of my brain, the squirrels running to the music. Obviously, it was time to get another beer and reflect on what to do next.

I sipped my second beer slowly and thought of an old *New Yorker* cartoon, one of my favorites. It showed an Amish-like father talking to his Amish-like son in a sparse room with hardwood floors under their feet and hardwood chairs hanging along the wall. The two were obviously in the middle of a serious father-son chat, and the son had just asked a question. In the caption, the father replies: "No, son, we're not Movers. We're just Shakers."

Now in my childhood, the reverse was true. Thanks to my father's restless spirit, if I had asked the same question, my father would have said we were *just Movers*. Unfortunately, we were the kind of Movers who were always renting or borrowing a truck, grabbing whatever empty boxes we could from neighbors, and drafting nearby relatives into a day's work as teamsters. My parents lived in more than forty different houses in the first fifty years of their marriage. In short, I was preconditioned by both nature and nurture not to stay put for very long. But shouldn't one's angst be more complex than a single-panel cartoon used as magazine filler?

Mexico has about as many towns named after Saint Michael, aka San Miguel, as America has towns named Long Beach, so it was necessary to add a second name to the San Miguel of the central highlands, in order to differentiate it from the many others and ensure that the right people spent their vacation in the San Miguel they expected, and not in a rustic village without plumbing by the same name. Toward that end, the name "Allende" was added, in honor of town native General Ignacio de Allende y Unzaga, one of the heroes of the Mexican War of Independence. It was thought, wisely perhaps, that christening the town after both a popular war hero and a revered saint would cover all bets with local authorities as well as a higher one.

More than four hundred and fifty years old, San Miguel de Allende is approximately a thousand feet higher than mile-high Denver, Colorado. Beautiful and historic, the town is justifiably considered one of Mexico's crown jewels. It was declared a national monument by the Mexican government in 1926, and, as a consequence of this honor, strict controls were immediately placed on its architecture, prohibiting such modern assaults on the human eye as glass buildings, neon signs, and traffic lights. To this day, the city, nearly smack dab in the middle of the country, remains charming and Mexican, regardless of those who complain it's too touristy or too American or too Canadian or too Starbucksy or too whatever. Of course, it doesn't hurt that the area is blessed with near-perfect weather, what the guidebooks refer to as "Eternal Spring."

Expats have flocked to San Miguel since the end of World War II, when the town was first pitched to those cashing in on their G.I. bills as an inexpensive place in which to study art. Previously, the town had struggled to find a regular source of revenue. But over the years, a handful of expats and Mexicans pulled together, worked hard, and helped put San Miguel back on the map, making it an attractive destination, especially for artistic types or those who preferred a squiggly line to a straight one. Neal Cassady, one of the Beat Generation's favorite sons, blew into town in 1968. According to local history, one cold night in February after one too many cold ones at a wedding party, this iconic beatnik decided to follow the train tracks to the next town. Wearing only a T-shirt and jeans, he didn't make it and was found the next morning in a coma, lying next to the tracks, dying a few hours later.

San Miguel has enjoyed or suffered, depending on one's perspective, an explosion of expat immigration. Along these lines, I'd been told about a phenomenon called "border promotion," which is a way of saying once you cross the southern border between the United States and Mexico, you can be anything you want. In other words, this is your chance to introduce yourself to others as "Admiral," even though your sea-going experience might be limited to managing a Skipper's franchise in Milwaukee. Part-time community theater actors are introduced as retired Off-Broadway performers. Likewise, Sunday choir singers become opera stars, and night school painters become the next soon-to-be-discovered Diego Rivera. The reality is, most expats don't care what anyone did on the other side of the border, so you might as well pad your, ahem, *curriculum vitae*. Personally, I think reinventing yourself is a good thing and more power to those who do it. As one friend suggested, another nickname for San Miguel could be the City of Second Acts.

The expat community in San Miguel de Allende consists mostly of Americans and Canadians. Out of nearly 100,000 city residents, and thousands more in the countryside, it's estimated that full- or part-time expats make up anywhere from 8,000 to 12,000, the number swinging widely depending on time of year or time of real estate closings. Although attempts to pinpoint exactly how many expats reside in San Miguel come and go, everyone agrees the majority of expats are escapees from the U.S., while a not so surprising large number of tourists are Mexican. San Miguel is a destination of great historic importance to the citizens of Mexico, and it's also known as a wild and crazy party town, a Mexicans Gone Wild sort of spot.

But what did it mean to be an expat? After nearly two years living as one, I still couldn't answer the question to my satisfaction. I knew the official meaning. According to today's democratic answer to Webster's dictionary, Wikipedia, an expatriate or expat is "a person temporarily or permanently residing in a country and culture other than that of the person's upbringing or legal residence." Okay, what about the guy from the United States pounding a San Miguel ATM and shouting: "Every time I punch in two hundred dollars, it gives me *pesos*. Why can't this thing talk to me in dollars?" Does even he qualify?

I began to think more and more about our expat experience. I wasn't looking for omens this time, only meaning and, perhaps, a modicum of understanding. I wanted to know, for example, why some expats succeeded where others failed. What distinguished a good expat from, say, a bad one? Were there any rules that should apply to an expat's life? Perhaps a David Letterman top ten list of "You know you're really an expat when..."? I didn't need to go to a guru with an advanced degree from an online university or a priest with a parish to find my answers, I thought. All I had to do was walk around town and pay closer attention than usual. So I did.

Known to some local residents as Jurassic Park, *El Jardin* is the town's principal plaza and serves as a *de facto* living room for expats. The square is covered in geometrically groomed trees, with open, bald tops like mysterious crop circles. Wrought iron benches surround a bandstand lodged in the park's mid-section. What one assumes are Spanish-speaking pigeons, as well as various colorful vendors shouting out or waving their wares, occupy the outer perimeter. At night, groups of mariachi bands add even more ambiance and sing romantic songs for a small fee, while young men and women, mostly boys and girls, stroll around the park and make eye-contact in the traditional Latin *paseo*, a froggy-goes-a-courting routine similar to "cruising Main" in the United States, only much slower and without having to stop for gas.

Benches in the park face the town's leading icon, *La Parroquia*, an impressive salmon-colored structure designed by an indigenous architect to resemble Gaudi's famous Barcelona cathedral, *Sagrada Família*, but on a much, much, much smaller scale. On most days, you'll find expats nesting on the benches, with the more seasoned expats occupying the best views of *La Parroquia* in a pecking order of sorts. During the off-season – the hot months or the wet months – life didn't get much better than my butt on a bench under a shady tree as I watched the parade of expats pass by. The only thing missing was background music by John Phillip Sousa.

During the course of a single afternoon I observed every main character type in town: from the aging faux blondes with handbags and small dogs in matching outfits to the unattached males, living frugally on low fixed incomes, to the wealthy expats, who would visit San Miguel a few times a year to check up on their third houses. I saw the nouveau artists, retired teachers or bankers or systems analysts painting in the great outdoors, in the *plein air* tradition of Monet and Van Gogh. Plenty of women with rolled up yoga mats and men with rolled up Cuban cigars walked by.

In general, the female expats wore anything and everything they wanted and typically draped themselves in wraps and shawls, like an Egyptian mummy, on top of loose cotton pants stitched in every color of the rainbow, a wild scarf protecting the chin, huge sunglasses covering the eyes, silver bangles on the wrists, and all topped off with a hat the size and shape of Idaho.

Many years earlier, when Arlene and I were in college and living together on next to nothing in a small house with cinder blocks for furniture and more books than food, she used to dress in such anarchistic fashion. It was refreshing back then, and I suppose it can be equally refreshing later in life, in a discovering-the-Fountain-of-Youth sort of way. One night during college, as Arlene was leaving to attend an evening class, I noticed she was dressed in a crazy quilt of clothes, well beyond even her normal slap-dash, Cost Plus, anything goes attire.

"I hope you get lost," I told her.

"Why would you say that?" she asked.

"Because I'd love to describe you to the police," I answered.

The male expats were much less imaginative and stuck mostly to baggy cargo pants, sandals or thick-soled hiking boots, and wide-brimmed hats. I must confess, my dress code was the least imaginative and most boring of all: regular fit jeans, a short-sleeved shirt, Ecco shoes, and a ball cap. I tried the wide-brimmed hat look, but it made me look like the Mayor of Munchkin City at a dude ranch. So it was back to my usual baseball cap, which enabled me to claim only two more inches of height, instead of six, but covered my bald spot, which was expanding faster than an Exxon oil slick, protected my eyes from the glaring sun, and shielded me in the rain. Not bad for under ten bucks.

I often wore a University of Oregon Ducks ball cap. It was a solid, dark green hat with a bright yellow big-O in the middle. One day, while walking up narrow, cobble-stoned Aldama Street in Centro to pick up our mail, I passed by someone working on a car, his head buried and out of sight. As I passed him, I heard the man say something in Spanish. Thinking he was talking to someone else, I proceeded up the hill. A few steps later what he'd said registered. It wasn't Spanish, it was English, and he'd said: "Go, Ducks!" I glanced back, but by then the man had disappeared under the car's hood.

But I digress from my survey of the Plaza. There were the big-hearted nonprofit volunteers sitting at a table and taking names, giving up their day to help feed the hungry, rescue stray dogs and cats, fund scholarships for students, or solicit petitioners against the latest American half-baked political excursion. I saw big-bellied eaters eager to debate the best place to go for *comida*. And New Age believers clutching bottles of prickly pear cactus on their way to or returning from a spiritual session with a shaman named Coyote Eyes, formerly known as Leonard Green from Pittsburgh. While sitting there once, I thought I overheard a couple of seventy-year-olds memorizing lines for the production of a local play, where he would play the young stud and she the ingénue.

On the one hand, it was truly inspiring to see how active seniors were in this town, where eighty was the new sixty and every day was an undisguised blessing. On the other, I can't help but recall the small party in our neighborhood early in our stay when Arlene was introduced to an older woman and found herself trapped in a typical expat conversation loop:

"How long have you lived in San Miguel?" the woman asked.

"Six months," said Arlene.

"Oh, you live in San Miguel?" the woman asked.

"Yes," said Arlene.

"How long have you lived here?"

"Six months."

"How long have you lived in San Miguel?"

"I said six months."

"Do you live here?" the woman repeated, still again.

"No," said Arlene, finally realizing a way out. "I'm just visiting."

With that, Arlene stepped away in time to hear the woman ask someone else how long the person had lived in San Miguel.

I could count more than 200 volunteer organizations run or supported by expats. Their efforts should not be understated. Arlene, for example, became part of the core group of an organization that raised money to provide scholarships to keep girls in school, from elementary school through college, thus helping to change the pattern of domestic violence and male dominance. One expat friend almost single-handedly saved a girls' orphanage from extinction and helped put it on a solid financial footing. Another expat friend rescued stray dogs from the town's streets, found doctors to heal and fix the dogs, then found homes for the wayward critters either in town or back in the States, even going so far as to fly them to their new owners. Still another expat friend co-founded a global organization in San Miguel that worked toward social justice and environmental sustainability. The list went on.

Expats also contributed money to the local economy simply by being there. They helped pay for the services of housekeepers, handymen, gardeners, waiters, restaurants, retail stores, gas stations, and so on. And, of course, expats also benefited from meeting and knowing each other. Living in San Miguel was a filtering process of sorts, and you were guaranteed to become acquainted with interesting, complex, and creative people, the more boring, risk-adverse types having stayed home in Sherman Oaks to play canasta or golf and watch reruns of "Dancing with the Stars."

Not everyone is cut out to succeed as an expat, whether in Mexico or elsewhere. If you love to eat breakfast early in the morning, expect vendors to show up to their appointments as scheduled, or jump out of your chair every time you hear a firecracker, then Mexico may not be your best option. If you prefer houses painted in muted tones and your roads smoothly paved, or if you liked new and squeaky clean instead of old and picturesque, you might want to abandon any thoughts of relocating south of the border.

But I had already jumped those hurdles. I was easy-going about breakfast and vendor appointments, and did my best to ignore the occasional blast of fireworks. I adored the colorful houses. In many ways, I was ready to embrace the expat experience and yet something was missing.

I wanted to feel part of such a select group, but it wasn't happening. Even if I started wearing a hat with a wider brim and traded my trusty standard for a toy poodle, I doubt my feelings would change. Simply put, I wasn't cutting it as an expat, and didn't know why. More and more I felt like the Martin Short character Ned in the film *The Three Amigos*, when he cried out: "What am I doing in Mexico?" Let's face it, some people are simply better suited for an extended stay at Epcot Center, where they can visit a dozen countries in the same afternoon and not have to mingle or deal with the locals. Was I in that group?

Back in the state of Oregon, I was having drinks in a bar with my friend Dan from the San Francisco Bay Area when a stranger sat down next to us. We introduced ourselves and learned the man was from Australia. The conversation turned to the experience of being a foreigner living in another country, and we asked how he liked living in the States.

He loved it, he said, adding that it wasn't easy at first. In fact, this was his second time living in America, and he went on to tell us about his initial foray as an expat, several years before, in San Francisco. He was a trained chef from Down Under and was looking forward to working in the beautiful food-savvy City by the Bay. Picking up the scene in the middle of the action, this is how the conversation unfolded:

Me: San Francisco? No kidding. I live in Portland now. Originally I'm from the Bay area. We're both from there.

Dan: East bay. Oakland.

Aussie: You're smart to stay on that side of the bay, mate. Much cheaper, you know, and safer.

Dan: Safer? (he chuckles, nearly choking on his drink)

Me: Where'd you live?

Aussie: Mission District.

Dan: That explains it. Dangerous place, the Mission.

Aussie: You got that right, mate. Two days after I move in I'm coming home from the bottle shop, you know. Got me a bag of groceries. All of a sudden, I hear gun shots. I duck and look around. Just down the street a guy's chasing another guy and shooting at him and they're heading my way.

Me: What'd you do?

Aussie: I run my ass off is what I do. Stuff starts falling out of one of my bags, then the other one ripped. I threw the bags down and picked up the pace.

He took a sip of his drink. We waited for him to continue.

Me: What else?

Aussie: So I reach my apartment building, you know, man. My hands are shaking but I unlock the door. Don't know how. My heart's coming out of my chest, you know, an' I race up to my room and open the door. Guess what happened next?

Me: What?

Aussie: My bloody phone's ringing. It's one of me cobbers from back home. I can't catch my breath. I'm gasping. He says, "Hello, mate, wot's it like in America?" I'm out of breath still, you know, and bloody gobsmacked, you know, still shaking like a friggin' leaf, I was. Didn't even have time for a smoke. So I take a deep breath to calm down, and then I scream into the bloody phone, "It's just like in the flippin' movies, mate. Just like in the movies!"

That chef got it. He took a life-threatening experience as an expat and gave it a positive spin. He survived and had a story to tell in a bar to two strangers. Maybe that's what I needed, and lacked. Why couldn't I be that resilient?

Alternative Use #15 for Nopals

Memoir of an Armoire

 *Concerning an evaluation of our time spent in Mexico in which I report certain conclusions jointly reached with a four percent margin of error, I decide to write a memoir, and we embark on a new adventure that turns out to be an old story after all*

God, she sure was gorgeous. She danced in, wearing a multi-colored, flowing skirt and an equally colorful scarf, pure passion on two legs. Silver bracelets dangled from her wrists. A hand-crafted necklace, as pigmented as a painter's swatch book, covered the glimpse of cleavage. Red, white, and green earrings bobbled on both sides of her face. Her smile sparkled, as she spotted me and sashayed over to my table.

This was not going to be easy. Our relationship had started on such a positive note, with great expectations on both sides.

I had ordered her favorite drink, mescal over ice, straight up, with two lime slices on the side, and it was waiting for her. For myself, I was already on my second nopal margarita. I walked over and kissed her on each cheek just as she was sitting down. I wavered long enough above her to take in a tangy whiff of hibiscus flower, her favorite perfume, then returned to my side of the table. I sat and took another sip.

She: Why'd you want to see me?

Me: We need to talk.
She: *Oh?*
Me: It's not working out.
She: What's not working out?
Me: Us.
She: What do you mean 'Us'? What'd I do wrong this time?
Me: Nothing. It's not you, it's me.
She: I hate when people say that.
Me: I think it might be time for us to part company.
She: You do?
Me: Yes. I've been giving it a lot of thought.
She: You know what your problem is? You never really tried.
Me: What's that supposed to mean?
She: Just how it sounded. We rarely talk. And it wouldn't matter because you never listen to what I say.
Me: I always listen. I just don't always understand you.
She: Wait a minute! Does this mean you no longer find me attractive?
Me: Not at all. I mean it doesn't mean that at all. You're beautiful and wonderful and you're always so much fun to be around. Every day you fill my heart with joy.
She: And you have a problem with that?
Me: I think so.
She: Really?
Me: I'd like us to still be friends.
She: I bet you would.
Me: Like I said, it's not you, it's me.
She: You bet it is.
She hurled my nopal margarita in my face, then stormed out, politely telling other diners "*Buen provecho*" as she exited.
The waiter brought me a hand towel.

"I thought that went well," I told him.

Hmm. Breaking up with Mexico would be the easy part, despite the waste of a good margarita. Now I had to explain it to Arlene, a task somewhere between a leap of faith and jumping off a cliff. But I didn't have to wait long.

Late one night in San Miguel I became violently ill, and by six the next morning I was flat on my back in the local hospital ER hooked up to IVs, a position I would maintain for more than ten hours. The next best thing to people-watching in *El Jardin* was spending ten hours on your back in the Emergency Room at Hospital de la Fe. Listening to the flow of hospital patients pass through on a typical day gave one a fairly balanced picture of a town's citizens. About half of the emergency patients were Mexican, the other half were expats. Babies were brought in for injections. Middle aged residents entered the hospital, worried they had suffered a heart attack. Speechless older folks were wheeled in, attended to, and then wheeled back out. It was a parade of illnesses, real and imagined.

In my own case, three weeks worth of meals either came up and out or down and out, as if someone had set off a stink bomb inside my body and everyone or everything had rushed for the nearest exit. Unwillingly, my elimination system had taken over and was in the process of getting rid of whatever my body thought it owned, a prices slashed, everything-must-go sale of food, drink, pills, alcohol, snacks, water, many things disgusting, more water, twigs, and strange stuff that looked like it was left over from the set of *Ghostbusters*. As they say, the works.

"If I were to die, would you stay in Mexico?" Arlene asked, sitting by my hospital bedside, as we both watched saline drip.

I thought about it for several seconds before replying, "No."

Then I returned the favor and asked Arlene if she would remain here, if I were to die while living in Mexico, a distinct possibility considering my condition at the time, and she also replied, "No."

Hmm. We looked at each other in silence, shrugged, and continued on to another topic. We didn't know it then, but answering that single question the way we did became a new tipping point, another defining moment, in our lives. We had lived in the middle of Mexico for nearly two years, but something wasn't right. It's possible we had hit the infamous two-year wall, a piece of artificial construction in expat lore that said after two years in San Miguel, no matter how fantastic the experience, you would get homesick.

All in all, life for us south of the border had been positive. But we missed family and friends back in the States, and we missed other aspects of our old life, tiny components one rarely considers and often takes for granted. For example, you can get wonderful chocolate and vanilla in Mexico, as well as the most ingenious combinations of ice cream. Mexican pastries are highly regarded and deservedly so.

But I'm a licorice kind of guy, and you just can't get a good rope of the basic red or black locally to save your soul. A year earlier we visited Arlene's sister in Las Vegas. We arrived at the airport, rented a car, and drove to the first drug store we could find to get something to relieve our allergies. It was a basic store, a Rite-Aid or Walgreens, some kind of chain that's in every neighborhood but, and here's my point, even though it was a basic store, it was full of stuff—the aisles were crammed with a gazillion products.

As we walked down an aisle, my eyes turned and, laser-like, zeroed in on one item. I grabbed a box of licorice from the shelf and held it up high in the air as if holding a bowling trophy on the last night of league play. Like some toothless resident of a small hollow deep inside of coal country, I screamed, "They got Red Vines, Arlene! They got Red Vines!"

Keeping my metaphor in the licorice section, after so many

years of Good & Plenty in America it was obvious we were spoiled and, ridiculous as it seemed, we missed the silly, meaningless, mass-marketed minutiae of our stateside life. For a time in Mexico, we felt what holes were left from our old existence were filled by a much simpler, more grounded lifestyle and the excitement of absorbing a different culture.

I thought of how our lives had changed, the slower pace, our gracious and friendly Mexican neighbors, the fascinating expats, annoying expats, supportive expats, the long unending stream of fiestas and festivals, the weather, always the weather. I even thought of the armoire we had purchased from an antiques shop. It was not what one might have expected to come upon in Mexico, either, and I'm sure if it could express emotion it would have been surprised to find itself so far from home. The armoire came from England and was covered, mural-like, with hand-painted illustrations from Lewis Carroll's Alice books, showing Alice and the Red Queen, as well as other characters. The piece was fun, well-executed, and appealed to the cartoonist in me. But how did it get here, I wondered, across the wide Atlantic to end up in the middle of Mexico? It was then I realized we all had stories to tell, what the film industry refers to as "backstory," even an armoire, and that's when I decided to throw my green and yellow cap into the writers' ring and pen (make that, keystroke) my own memoir. I thought doing so might help me better understand this unusual chapter in our lives. I had already finished a couple of essays, along with several long, anecdotal stories in emails to friends. A memoir might be the ticket.

And why not? Even if I didn't get everything right, it wouldn't matter. Charles Barkley, the NBA star, once complained during a press conference that he had been misquoted in his autobiography. Besides, it seemed as if every expat in San Miguel was working on, had already finished, or was considering writing his or her memoir. Our expat friend and neighbor George, for example, was planning a three-volume set of his life. When I reminded him even Benjamin Franklin only had one autobiographical volume to his credit, George shrugged, chuckled, and said, "Ben Franklin never partied with Sinatra and The Rat Pack."

Good point. In his early years, I think my friend was present at the birth of sex, drugs, and rock an' roll. Besides, I found George to be one of the funniest men in town. I didn't doubt his wicked sense of humor could keep readers laughing, shaking their heads, or both through three books.

Yet, after nearly two years of living in Mexico, Arlene and I had doubts whether we were cut out for life as full-time expats. We wondered if we were not better suited for the seasonal three-month stay, either during the winter as *snowbirds* or the summer as *sweatbirds*.

To be sure, San Miguel was a soft landing and we had experienced an amazing adventure, with absolutely no regrets for the time we spent in Mexico, and would recommend a similar adventure to anyone, no matter their age, wishing to change his or her life, and willing to drop everything to do so. At first we knew no one and could barely speak the language; now we had friends there and could speak Spanish with the fluency of a slow three-year-old. I would miss, for example, the many opportunities to say *jacaranda* and *jicama* in the same sentence. But, as a previous employer used to say when layoffs were coming, sacrifices had to be made.

Because Arlene and I believe you can't go home again, once we move away from an area we never move back. We return to visit, of course, but never again to live there. We feel life's too short. The world is too interesting. There are simply too many towns and cities and not enough days or dollars to see them all. So this time we set our sights on the original hometown of Thomas Wolfe's "you can't go home again" theory: Asheville, North Carolina. We were moving back to the States, to *Estados Unidos*, to a new and different place in *El Norte*. Once again, we were ready to dust off our pet carriers, pack our luggage, and set our Audi steering wheel to an uncharted course, north-east. And yes, once again, we would be strangers in a strange land. More importantly, the adventure would live on.

Or would it?

Timing and a good sauce are everything, and our timing in crossing the border and re-entering the U.S. was atrocious, ranking in the lower ten percentile of good timing scores. We crossed during a storm, with high winds and water whipping us every which way but loose and visibility reduced to a few car lengths. Not only that, our Audi was showing signs of overheating.

"How can it overheat?" Arlene asked. "We're in the middle of a hurricane?"

"Tropical storm, and it's the tail end," I corrected.

"Do we need to stop at a gas station?"

"Not now. Let's wait until we cross and spend the night in Laredo, let the car cool down first and then see."

"Is this an omen?" Arlene asked.

"What do you mean?"

"All this rain and the car acting up?"

"Yeah, so?"

"Maybe someone's telling us we shouldn't be leaving Mexico," she suggested.

"I don't believe in omens," I countered.

"Since when?"

"Since about six months after we moved to San Miguel. If you're not careful, everything becomes an omen. Besides, looking for omens is counter-productive. All it does is raise your blood pressure."

"I'm impressed," said Arlene.

"I'd rather let stuff happen and then deal with it, instead of worrying about things before they happen. I'm taking a more relaxed approach to life," I said.

"Relaxed? You're a worry wart. You can't help yourself."

"Not any more. *De nada* is my new mantra," I said, smiling.

"Really?"

"Really."

"I'm shocked."

"But I still believe in luck. And we're going to need plenty of it to reach Asheville. The car's falling apart," I said.

"He's back!" Arlene replied.

"Who's back?"

"Mr. Negative," said Arlene. "For a second there I thought I'd lost you."

Minutes later a U.S. agent in a wet rain slicker waved us across the Columbia bridge border crossing and we were back in the USA, where we made our way to Laredo for the night. The next morning, after only two hours on the road, the thermostat started to rise above the safe mid-point. I split my time between watching the road and the temperature gauge, my stomach acids churning like the boiler room on the *Titanic*. After only five hours on the road, we pulled in and spent the night in Houston.

The next day, I couldn't keep my eyes off the dashboard. Attention to detail didn't matter because just outside of Gulfport, Mississippi, the Audi finally broke down. Stuck in highway traffic on a drenching, humid July day, our noble steed began steaming until it barely ran at all. Powerless, I watched the thermostat slowly inch its way north of the mid-point all morning.

Gasping and quivering, the car finally said, "*No mas.*" If we were in a Western movie, I would have pulled out my gun and shot it in the head gasket. Instead, we rolled into the first motel in Gulfport we could find, checked in, and called the nearest Audi dealership, which was in Mobile, Alabama, a daunting fifty-five miles to the east. They told us they would send a tow service to pick up our car in the morning.

Meanwhile, I asked the desk clerk at the motel if he could recommend a restaurant for dinner that evening. Without looking up, the clerk said, "The Blowfly Inn, just across the street." How strange, I thought. When I was in the U.S. Navy and assigned to the Seabees more than thirty years before, I was stationed in Gulfport and my favorite restaurant was The Blowfly Inn. Back then the restaurant had only one location, and it was in the middle of bayou country, not the middle of town, off a dirt road and not off a major interstate highway. In fact, it was the kind of charming dive-like place that had Fats Waller on the jukebox and Volkswagens with gun racks in the parking lot. More to the point, as I recalled, it offered a delicious steak dinner. Tired, hungry, and desperate for a quiet evening away from the pets, as soon as we could, we rushed over to the restaurant. Our expectations were sky high.

Unfortunately I had forgotten a low point about the food presentation at The Blowfly Inn, which obviously didn't matter to me when I was in the military but made a difference in civilian life.

"What's this?" Arlene said, looking at her plate in disgust.

"What do you mean?" I asked.

"There are plastic flies on my plate," she said.

"Not just any plastic flies. Blowflies," I said, as if that mattered.

"I don't care," Arlene said. "It's gross."

"It's just marketing, Arly. It's part of their theme," I said, again as if that mattered.

"Hmm," said Arlene.

"They're not real flies. They're plastic," I argued.

"I don't care if they're made of chocolate, they're flies!"
"But they're not real."
"They look real."
"Don't look at them."
"I can't *not* *look* at them. They're all over my plate."
"Well, then, just take them off your plate. They're not going to fly away on their own."
"I'm not hungry," she said, pushing her plate away. "I think I'll have another drink."

Later I looked up "blowfly" online and, once again, I had to admit Arlene was right. The definition literally steals one's appetite. Apparently, the large, metallic-colored blowfly lays its eggs on meat, which is not exactly the kind of three-star presentation of a ribeye that's going to win the coveted title of master chef. Nonetheless, I ate and enjoyed my meal for it was, indeed, the same restaurant and the steak was even better than my memory, which isn't saying much since I suffer from CRS syndrome, or Can't Remember Shit. After Hurricane Katrina wiped out the original restaurant the owners relocated to a new, temporary spot, which happened to be adjacent to our motel, while waiting for the diner to be resurrected at its old location. My old self would have considered it an omen.

In the morning a tow truck driver arrived with a flatbed truck. Arlene, Cassie, and I fit inside the cab of the truck, along with the driver, with Cassie sitting on our laps. Unfortunately, there was no room in the cab for Sadie, so she had to ride in her crate in the Audi, strapped to the flatbed.

During the 55-mile drive to the Audi dealership, we'd occasionally look back at our Audi and watch it bounce up and down, as if it were on a trampoline. Flap, flap, flap. We swore we could hear Sadie answering "Meow" with each flap. Flap. Meow. Flap. Meow. Flap. Meow… for 55 miles! When we finally arrived at our motel in Mobile, Sadie scurried under the bed and did not emerge for two days. We couldn't blame her. We did the same thing. Arlene and I emerged only long enough for meals, hunkering down like newly inducted members into the Witness Protection Program.

Then, one morning, four days later we got the call.

"Our car's ready?" I repeated, incredulously.

The mechanic on the other line laughed before answering. "Yes, sir. That's what I said. It's ready. But I got to tell y'all something."

"What's that?" I asked.

He chuckled again before answering. It was a polite laugh, but almost nervous at the same time.

"There were hoses missing and things just not right inside. If you know what I mean."

"I'm afraid I don't know what you mean."

"You work on the car yourself?"

"No."

"Some other mechanic, then?"

"Why do you ask?"

"Well, someone messed around with your engine real good."

"In what way?"

"They disconnected hoses, duct-taped some things. Turned other things off, too. Where you guys coming from?"

"Mexico."

"I'm surprised y'all made it this far," he said.

"Did you fix it?"

"Yes, sir. Y'all can come by any time now and pick up your car."

I had a flashback to the gas pump guy in Portland and his omen. Then I thought of Jesús, my neighborhood mechanic, and the miracles he had performed. If he had to disconnect a hose or two to keep us running, well then so be it. Our trusty *Rocinante* had performed above and beyond the call of road duty, and I felt lucky to have made it to Mexico and back out again all in one piece. The precison-engineered German Audi proved ill-designed for life in the middle of loosey-goosey Mexico.

We arrived in Asheville expecting to sign the final papers and move into the condo we were building. Prior to our arrival, the builder had guaranteed our condo would be finished and we'd be able to move in right away. We contacted him several times, from Mexico and the road, where he reiterated there were no problems and our condo would be ready, on time, as planned.

It wasn't ready, of course, so we stayed at a motel that accepted pets, one that included a refrigerator and a two-burner stove. Best of all, the motel was air-conditioned. As it turned out, we made it to Asheville in time for the hottest, most humid August on record. All four of us would huddle over the air conditioning vent, sucking priceless cool air with the intensity of someone who had just escaped a house fire. After four weeks of motel life in Asheville, a charming mountain town with wonderful art deco buildings, we couldn't handle the humidity or the wait and negotiated out of the contract. We went home again to Portland, Oregon.

The country of Mexico is vast and close, friendly and harsh, beautiful and difficult. It's a developing country and still a work in progress after centuries, one that faces huge educational and economic hurdles, drug violence, and political corruption, just to name four of its more important challenges. It's possible, one hundred years from now, the same thing will be said, because time and change in Mexico are strange concepts.

Mexico's true strength, however, is its people, especially the close-knit families who, when it comes to promoting family values, actually do walk the talk. If the average Mexican family had as much money as it has heart, such families would be among the richest on Earth. Maybe they already are and the rest of us don't know it. What I do know is that it was our great pleasure to live among them for two years, and we looked forward to returning some day.

Nobody Knows the Spanish I Speak

Guests

Epilogue Cassidy Rides Again

 *Regarding how at long last our story reaches a conclusion, of sorts, even if it does come full circle and I'm still not sure what any of it means*

So Thomas Wolfe was wrong. You can go home again—and again and again. And if things have changed and home looks different the second or third time around, well, man up and get over it.

Almost three years after we returned to live in the United States, we found ourselves, incredulously, perhaps miraculously, crammed inside another small car, this time a Nissan Versa, with a dog and a cat and whatever we could fit of their belongings and ours, driving back to Mexico. Simply put, we missed the place and, in Tony Bennett fashion, had left our hearts in San Miguel.

It didn't hurt Mexico's cause that in Portland rainfall records were falling like hackneyed cats and dogs. Our bodies creaked more than the Tin Man's metal torso; whenever we moved, we were a special effect for a radio ghost story.

Plus, re-entry into the USA was more difficult than we anticipated. We found life expensive and challenging with each passing day, our anxiety level was much higher, and the pace of living was too fast for us, even in laid-back Portland.

So what was different for us this time? We had lost our beloved Cassie two years earlier to cancer and only recently had acquired another standard poodle. This time we ended up with an 80-pound apricot-colored male, a big dog even by "standard" standards. His name is Duke and he was nearly four years old when we got him. Friends suggested we change his name, but somehow "Duke" fit him to a T-bone. Like Cassie, he looks regal when he wants to, but most of the time he's so easy-going he reminds us of the "Dude" in *The Big Lebowski*. We often refer to him as "His Dukeness" and "El Dukerino" and sometimes, when we're into that brevity thing, just "The Duke" because, as in the movie, this dog abides.

Duke takes up one half of the backseat, the other half going to Sadie, who had softened over the three years and no longer viewed humans as scratching posts. During this next drive down, Sadie would give us the same problems every morning as before, playing hide and go seek, but once in the car she was always the perfect passenger, with only the occasional "Meow," as justified, to reflect her disapproval of my driving.

For the most part, our drive south and east and south again was as uneventful as our first venture five years earlier. That's not to say we didn't hit a few speed bumps along the way. Just outside of Portland, we drove through a tornado watch, for example, a rare weather event in the Pacific Northwest. We negotiated our way through falling snow in the mountains and battled heavy winds in the Southwest. We stayed in the same cheap, pet-friendly motels and ate at the same disgusting local diners. We followed the same boring route, all as before.

My sole excitement came when I noticed a highway sign during a very long, desolate stretch of flat road in the Southwest. The sign read: "Dust May Exist." I thought how refreshing it was to see those words along the side of the road, an existential question of the highest ontological order. Yes, dust may exist. Then again, it may not.

Travel in Mexico had changed, too, since our last trek and not necessarily for the better. Stories abounded in the U.S. press and over the Internet about shakedowns and shootouts, particularly along the northern border. When we told our Portland friends we were driving back to Mexico, they stared wide-eyed. "Isn't it dangerous?" they'd ask. "Driving from the Texas border to San Miguel takes ten hours," I'd answer, calmly. "It's just like driving from Portland to Sacramento... only with people shooting at you."

But nobody shot at us. Nobody strip-searched us at the border. And nobody jacked our car. With so many newer, bigger, and more expensive makes and models to choose from, it would have taken a car jacker with very low self-esteem or poor eyesight to choose our white, fuel-efficient Nissan from the parade of vehicles making their way south. Easing our road trip worries, an expat couple who were much more experienced in traveling in Mexico generously offered to let us follow them from the border to San Miguel. Gladly, we took them up on their offer.

We also shared the road with fast drivers and *federales* at security stops, as well as armed and ski-masked men who may or may not have been *federales* at rest stops. The highway lanes were still tight, with little or no shoulder to offer comfort in case of an emergency. At one security checkpoint, I was asked by a heavily armed guard to open the trunk, which I did, smiling the whole time. As if on cue, Duke's metal food bowl rolled out and landed at his feet. The man stared at the bowl for a moment, then looked at all the dog and cat food, the cat's litter box, the dog's bed, their toys, the whole pet megillah. He shook his head as if making a comment to himself about stupid gringos and their spoiled pets. I imagine he had to justify pulling us over, so he pointed to some meaningless papers with the tip of his semi-automatic weapon and asked if that was our documentation for the *mascotas*, our pets? I replied with a confident "*Sí*" and another reassuring smile. He waved us on our way.

Just before dusk we arrived in one piece, dusty and smelly and exhausted, at the house of dear friends in our old neighborhood of La Lejona. We'd rented a place closer to the center of town this time, but it wasn't ready yet. Our friends had a delicious home-cooked meal waiting for us, including plenty of wine, and we were finally able to relax. Oddly enough, although we were tired of the drive and of each other, we felt as if we had come home.

The next morning I woke up to discover someone had stolen our hubcaps. I told Arlene *de nada* and wrote it off as nothing more than a fraternity hazing, the price one pays for admission to an elite club. Besides, who needs hubcaps in paradise?

Nobody Knows the Spanish I Speak

One Day in Bernal

Postscript

 *In which after our return to San Miguel I share more thoughts in something known as a postscript, which doesn't have anything to do with Post-it Notes, Post Toasties or software by Adobe Systems*

The year is 2011. Since the first time Arlene and I lived in San Miguel, the town has changed. It's now a full-fledged, card-carrying, flag-waving UNESCO World Heritage Site. The power lines that once draped the center of town with a confusion of wires have been relocated underground, not all but most. Dogs still run wild in the streets, but thanks to the generous efforts of canine rescue groups there are fewer homeless critters than before. More people wear shorts in town, thanks to a relaxed dress code. The two traffic lights are gone, the buses freshly painted, the green taxis more prevalent, and art galleries still rule. Restaurants are more diverse than ever, and the town recently opened its first five-star hotel, catering to fewer American tourists but more Mexican ones.

Dancing is alive and well at an Arthur Murray studio. And the live theater scene has improved dramatically, pun intended, with the best deal in town still being the Playreaders Theater series, where for under two dollars you get an evening of top-notch staged readings. The number of fully staged performances has mushroomed as well. Shortly after our return, we attended two separate plays by Players Workshop, a new theater company since our last stay, and had our respective socks knocked off. Speaking of socks and getting knocked off, I have yet to encounter another scorpion, but we no longer check our bed at night or shoes in the morning. Who says we don't live on the edge?

Organic food has made its way to San Miguel, in the form of several organic food stores and a weekly organic farmers' market. I can buy licorice at a cool cheese shop, just around the corner from where we live, and we can get *The New York Times* delivered to our doorstep daily, if we so choose. In one of the more noticeable changes, we no longer find ourselves stalled behind a slow-moving truck on a twisting, narrow mountain pass when making a Costco run to Celaya. That singular thrill is gone, since a new, wider, and much safer road was put in.

My story was a simple one. I suppose if I had lived my entire life in Omaha, Nebraska, and at the age of 55 decided to drop out, sell everything, and move to Manhattan, where I didn't know a soul and could barely speak the language, I would have told a similar tale of ineptitude. And I could have titled my book, "Nobody Knows the Yiddish I Speak." But my story took place—and continues—in the magical town of San Miguel de Allende, Mexico, a soft landing for expats to be sure. Nonetheless, leaving your job, selling everything, and moving to another country, without the safety net of a home back in the States or an employer looking out for your welfare or understanding more than a few phrases of the native language, was a big leap for us. We moved there. We left there. We returned there.

Did I learn anything the first time around? I hope so. If I had to reduce the rules of expat life to one word, that word would be "respect." You've chosen to live as a guest in someone else's country. It's absurd to complain about the differences from your country of origin or expect the ATM's to cough up your withdrawal in U.S. dollars. The second word, if I were pushed by the mainstream media to add a follow-up response, would be "cherish." Cherish the experience, not just the ups but the downs as well. Smile a lot, tip generously, and occasionally take a stab at using the local language. I plan to study Spanish again, even though I'm too old to master anything other than a clipped expression or two. All in all, being a stranger in a strange land can be immensely rewarding, if you let it.

Well, that's my story and I'm sticking to it. If it has offended anyone, I sincerely apologize. The offense rests entirely on my slouched shoulders. All compliments may be sent to my publisher. Please send any complaints to the American consulate in Düsseldorf.

The world is an amazing place. ¡Viva La Humanidad!

There are ten thousand memoirs in the City of Fallen Women. This was one of them.

About the Author

Ahem. In all modesty...

Mark Saunders, an award-winning playwright, screenwriter, and cartoonist, worked in high-tech and flirted briefly with stand-up comedy, performing in smoke-filled biker bars for loud drunks and late-night janitors. He once owned a Yugo (don't ask). Mark lives with his wife, writer Arlene Krasner, in San Miguel de Allende, Mexico. *Nobody Knows the Spanish I Speak* is his first book. He recently published *Dogs, Cats & Expats,* his second book and a sequel of sorts.

Knish Books

Our focus as Knish Books is in two general areas of interest: food writing and humor writing. Or, as we like to say, food that makes you smile and laughs that make you hungry. Knish Books is based in the beautiful colonial city of San Miguel de Allende, Mexico, selected by Condé Nast Traveler magazine as the "Best Small City in the World." Visit our website, knishbooks.com, for a light and tasty literary nosh.

Kosher Sutra by Arlene Krasner

A food memoir about the author's search for a meaningful life, ill-equipped as she was at times to articulate what that truly meant. Yet when all else failed—her career, her marriage, her much-adored but silly-looking AMC Gremlin—she could always rely on her love of food, running the table from comfort food to nouvelle cuisine. *Kosher Sutra* is a wonderful palate cleanser that fits sweetly and nicely between the courses of Oy vey and Mazel tov. Don't just change your life... change a recipe!

> "After reading *Kosher Sutra*, you'll think an old friend popped back into your life for a few days and feel a little miffed that she didn't stay longer."
> Foster Church, Pulitzer Prize-winning author of *Discovering Main Street*

Dogs, Cats & Expats by Mark Saunders. In this long-awaited sequel to the humorous memoir *Nobody Knows the Spanish I Speak*, which turns out not to be a sequel after all, Saunders shares his thoughts and experiences, mostly funny and a few more serious, in this collection of 30 essays about dogs, cats, and his life as a clueless expat living in the middle of Mexico.

"Don't read this book! Unless you want to laugh. Then by all means read this book! Mark Saunders offers you the unvarnished truth. Take him up on it!"
David Temple, author of *Five Times Lucky* (Winner of the 2021 American Fiction Award for Comedy)

Nobody Knows the Spanish I Speak

Discussion Guide

Behind the Author

An award-winning playwright, screenwriter, and cartoonist, Mark Saunders tried standup comedy to get over shyness and failed spectacularly at it—the standup part, not the shyness. He once owned a Yugo and still can't remember why. Nearly 30 of his plays have been staged, from California to New York—with several stops in-between—and two plays have been published. With three scripts optioned, his screenplays, all comedies, have attracted awards but seem to be allergic to money.

Back in his drawing days, more than 500 of his cartoons appeared nationally in publications as diverse as *Writer's Digest*, *The Twilight Zone Magazine*, and *The Saturday Evening Post*. As a freelancer, he also wrote gags for the popular comic strip "Frank and Ernest," as well as jokes for comedians, including Jay Leno.

Behind the Book

In early December of 2005, the author and his wife, along with their dog and cat, packed up their 21st century jalopy, a black

Audi Quattro with a luggage carrier on top, and left Portland, Oregon, for San Miguel de Allende, three thousand miles away in the middle of Mexico, where they knew no one and could barely speak the language.

Things fell apart almost from the beginning. The house they rented was as cold as a restaurant's freezer. Their furniture took longer than expected to arrive. They couldn't even get copies of their house keys made. They unintentionally filled their house with smoke and just as unintentionally knocked out the power to their entire neighborhood.

In other words, they were clueless. *Nobody Knows the Spanish I Speak* is their story.

Questions

1. The author and his wife were inspired by the Joseph Campbell quote: "Follow your bliss." How do you define *bliss*? Do you think the couple found it? Have you ever attained bliss in your life (surviving either an IRS audit or Thanksgiving with the in-laws doesn't count)? If so, what made that time or event so special or blissful?

2. As they begin their journey, the author encounters three "salted omens." Are the omens to be taken seriously? What happens eventually to his omen belief system? Can you recall an event in your life that you felt was preceded by a salted omen or even one without salt?

3. Have you ever wanted to reinvent yourself, even though someone else might already own the patent? Do you think such re-invention is possible? If you could "re-invent" yourself, how would you describe your new identity to others and how do you think they would react?

4. What is a "border promotion?" Do you know anyone who has ever given herself or himself a border promotion without moving to another country? Have you ever stretched the truth about your experience? What is the line between justifiable self-promotion and not telling the truth?

5. The book's title conveys that the book will be a story about miscommunication. What examples of miscommunication do you recall from the book? From your own life? (Please clearly communicate your answer to others.) How did you resolve or respond to your miscommunication episodes?

6. The author has issues with scorpions that interfere with his REM sleep. Can you think of other issues that kept him up at night? Does the author worry needlessly? Is worrying an emotion or an affliction? If you don't want to answer this set of questions, don't worry about it.

7. After reading this book, what did you find to be the author's overall perception of his life in Mexico? Have you ever visited Mexico and, if so, what was your impression?

8. Mark Twain called humor "man's greatest blessing." James Thurber said, "Humor is emotional chaos remembered in tranquility." How would you define humor? Now that you're enjoying some tranquility, name three humorous events in your life (not that three, the other three) and explain what was so funny about each event.

9. What is an expat? Are there good expats and bad expats? Have you ever lived for an extended period of time in a foreign country? If you could establish a set of rules, a Miss Manner's expat

etiquette, what expat rules would you establish and how would you enforce them?

10. Don't give up now. It's our final question and it's for all the money. What life lessons, if any, did the author and his wife learn from their adventure?

Thank you for your patience. Remember to get your parking ticket stamped by the receptionist on your way out. *¡Vaya con nachos!*

For Further Reading:
- *Solamente en San Miguel, Volume 1,* edited by Cris K.A. DiMarco
- *Solamente en San Miguel, Volume 2,* edited by Jeanne Mills
- *On Mexican Time* by Tony Cohan
- *Flirting in Spanish* by Susan McKinney de Ortega
- *Falling... in Love With San Miguel* by Carol Schmidt and Norma Hair

Online Sites about San Miguel de Allende:
- http://portalsanmiguel.com/
- http://www.bibliotecasma.com/
- http://www.vivasanmiguel.com/
- http://www.exploreandgomexico.com/

www.ingramcontent.com/pod-product-compliance
Lightning Source LLC
LaVergne TN
LVHW041331080426
835512LV00006B/398